Sales Leadership

Distinctions With A Difference

Wayne
15 Dec 2015

Sales Leadership

Distinctions With A Difference

Wayne Fredin

Published by Action Leadership Inc.

2015

First Printing: 2015

ISBN 978-0-9948000-0-8

Action Leadership Inc.
Suite 433, 505-8840 210 Street
Langley, British Columbia, Canada, V1M2Y2

www.actionleadership.ca

Dedication

To my loving wife Maureen
Without your patience and support
This would not ever have been completed

Contents

Acknowledgements 1

Introduction 3

Section 1 – Fundamental Leadership 9

Setting the Stage 10

Principle #1 - Leadership Must Be Visible 12

Principle #2 - Lead By Example... 14

Principle #3 - Leaders Must Know What It Like To Be Led 16

Principle #4 - Are You Decisive Or Impulsive? 18

Principle #5 - Be Irrelevant And Not Irreverent To Your Success ... 20

Principle #6 - The 3 Legged Stool Of Leadership............................. 22

Principle #7 - Business Not Personal 24

Principle #8 - Leading Leaders Versus Leading Followers 26

Principle #9 - Leadership Is Not An 8-5 Job 27

Principle #10 - Share Success And Accept Blame 28

Leadership Versus Management 29

Section 1 Bonus – A Decision Making Process.................................. 33

Section 2 – Sales Leadership Challenges....................................... 39

Background 40

Challenge #1 – Everyone Believes They Can Sell! 41

Challenge #2 – Your Boss Used To Be A Sales Leader 44

Challenge #3 – You Have Hiring But Not Firing Authority 47

Challenge #4 – Some Of Your Sales Team Are Protected Or Untouchable.... 49

Challenge #5 –Making The Inside Sale 51

Challenge #6 – Dealing With Multiple Offices And Staff 53

Challenge #7 – Dealing With The Purchase Order Prevention Department.. 55

Challenge #8 – Creating And Managing The Forecast....................... 57

Challenge #9 – Targets! 60

Challenge #10 – Sales Team Are Too Busy To Actually Sell 62

Challenge #11 – Group Or Individual Meetings And How Often? 65

Challenge #12 – Selling Versus Business Development 67

Challenge #13 – Selling Or Business Development Versus Account
Management 69

Challenge #14 – Who Owns The Customer? 71

Challenge #15 – Chasing Money!..73

Challenge #16 – Who Owns Price And Margin? 74

Challenge #17 – I Need It Today!..76

Challenge #18 – What Is A Good Sales Call?...................................77

Challenge #19 – Joint Sales Calls For Mentoring And Coaching.................79

Challenge #20 – Managing The Training Gap.................................81

Challenge #21 – Having An Effective And Efficient CRM 82

Challenge #22 – Which Came First – Your Sales Process Or Your CRM?.......83

Challenge #23 – How Do You Manage Really Long Sales Cycles? 84

Challenge #24 – Selling Vapourware – Cannibalizing Your Sales 86

Challenge #25 – How Do You Manage Competitive Differentiation?............87

Section 3 - Sales Thoughts and Ideas..92

Planning 94

Key Accounts..105

Team Player 114

Sales Basics...124

Process And Prospecting 162

Closing...177

Dealing With Adversity 184

Be A Great Example...201

Elevate And Motivate...216

Section 4 – My Top 10 254

Section 5 - Notes...259

Acknowledgements

Thanks to the 1980 graduating class from Royal Roads Military College. Bert, Clayton, Doug, Jim, Ken, Klaus, Mark, Paul, Pierre and Steve; it all started with you on August 14th, 1976.

Thanks to many friends and colleagues who coached, mentored and inspired me to grow as a person and encouraged me to write this book. Debra and Alan, Patrick, Ian and Judy, Bill and Nuala, Joan and Merv and many more too countless to name – you made a difference to me and I will always be thankful.

Thanks to my Dad and late Mom who always encouraged me to strive and grow and my brother Terry who in recent years has become a great friend and confidant.

Introduction

I have been planning to write this book for too many years to admit. Back in 1988 while a student on what was known as Technical Staff (read Project Management) Training at the Royal Military College of Science at Shrivenham England, I coined a phrase that has effectively become my personal creed ever since. Somewhere in my personal files I still have the paper attested to by a classmate who was, at the time, a Major in the Royal Australian Army where I wrote 'Management is the Science of Reaction, Leadership is the Art of Action'. At the time, the British Army was significantly challenged with both delays and overspending on many of their key capital programs and was introducing new processes and technologies to better manage their defence budgets. We were lectured to by both operational and procurement leaders and managers on the need to better manage the Crown coin. It seemed like every guest speaker up to and including 3 star generals said "If you cannot measure it, you cannot manage it" or words to that effect. Having spent the majority of my military career to that point in operationally focussed combat units, I found this management philosophy quite disconcerting. It was only later on after spending time in the Ottawa project management meat grinder that I began to understand what was really being taught and why but more on that later..

In the past 35 years I have followed 4 major careers and truly believe I am multi-dimensional as a result of these life experiences. I have been a highly committed Army Officer, I have been self-employed in business including at one point with my Father, I have worked for major corporations in junior and mid management roles and I have been an Executive in both public and private companies. I also had the privilege of serving as a part time Reserve officer in both staff and command roles for 13 years until retiring recently and this, like all my other experiences, has shaped my views and opinions on Leadership.

The fundamental principles, philosophies and beliefs that form the basis of this book are rooted in my background and experiences. As a cadet and student at Royal Roads Military College in the 70s I was subjected to very standard and traditional military leadership training. Some might call it

5

a form of brainwashing and it probably was, but not in a negative sense; in addition to a normal academic curriculum we were subjected to a constant diet of formal classes actually called Military Leadership and Management, drill, senior or upper classman in positions of authority and on and on which shaped my early development in preparation to becoming an officer.

After four years in the Military College system and summers at my Signals specific training I was finally ready to be given my first job as an officer in command of what we referred to as professional and volunteer soldiers. That was a real wakeup call! Leadership theory is one thing and practical experience where you have some pseudo authority over your peers is another, but true command is quite something else. Over the next nine years I held six different positions ranging from Troop Officer and Platoon Commander of up to 35 soldiers, junior staff officer, operations officer, full time student and senior staff officer. In these roles I continued to have my views and opinions on leadership and management strongly influenced, sometimes positively by incredibly talented and effective people but just as often by others whose style, approach, demeanor and the like taught what not to do.

In 1989 I resigned my commission and joined SHL Systemhouse in Ottawa, my first but not last foray into the world of big business in general and sales in particular. What was fascinating to me was the complete lack of the term leadership in corporate communications or jargon; at that time it was all about management and administration. As bureaucratic as the military was at least the rules, regulations, procedures and processes were well defined and written down and when confused you could ask for help. In the corporate world these were all 'muddy waters' and there may have been a couple of long term people who could offer some advice but for the most part it was poorly defined, poorly documented and poorly managed. It was in this environment that I learned about 'knowledge brokering', something that I have fundamental challenges with but more on that later.

I left Systemhouse to chase my dreams as an Independent Contractor (self-employed) in the Network Marketing industry. Although I was in a

Sales role at Systemhouse I never really admitted that because in Ottawa everyone in Sales carries other titles like Consultant or Business Development. My first true experiences and lessons as a Salesman came from me doing direct sales calls when the option was to make Sales or find another salary based job! I also quickly realized that significant income was only possible by building and developing a team and so I did that as well. It was here that I was able to hone my Coaching, Mentoring and Leadership skills. Having started in the military, where whoever has more rank wins, to an environment where everyone is self-employed so there is no superior to subordinate relationship, yet the effects of quality leadership can have a massive impact, forced me to rethink what true leadership is all about.

For the past almost thirteen years I have been in various sales, sales management and sales leadership roles in both private and public companies. For eight of these years, I have been the senior sales person totally responsible for the performance of geographically dispersed sales teams. Perhaps the key lesson learned from these years has been that everyone believes they know how to sell and they all want their opinions to count; the truth is many of them either have no pure sales training or experience or it is so dated to be almost irrelevant. Often caught in the middle as a member of the Executive Team but still a Sales guy in practice and at heart, the mantle of Sales Leader takes on a whole new meaning with a set of challenges that some days seem insurmountable.

This book is the sum total of my experiences as a Leader, Mentor, Coach and Sales Professional. I offer it simply as a resource that I hope you are able to take advantage of to improve your quality of life in your career, position or profession. Am I independently wealthy? Not yet. Did I rise to the rank of General Officer or CEO in the Military or Civilian world? No. Having admitted that, I do believe that my personal journey has offered me unique insight into many of the key attributes of Sales Leadership and so I present this book as a collection of lessons and anecdotes for you to internalize and contemplate next time you are faced with a challenge or dilemma.

Section 1 –
Fundamental
Leadership

Setting the Stage

Leadership has become a buzzword of the 21st Century. Every university and college boasts and promotes some type of leadership program. While these all offer value, my personal perspective is there is no substitute for real world experience; let me present an example of what I mean. Have you ever pointed out to someone that the metaphorical road they are on is full of obstacles and tried to offer advice on how to navigate around them to hear something like "thanks for your ideas but I am okay?" This is human nature. Later you find out that this person went down the road and tripped over an obstacle or two before they figured they should maybe have listened to you the first time around. This is normal because to this individual your advice was all theoretical, whereas their personal experience was very much practical.

Don't get me wrong; I really enjoy reading books from world and business leaders who have had a significant impact in their 'community'. What I tend to do is look for opportunities to use the lessons learned from these masters and apply them into my real day to day situations, tempering them against previous experiences and perspectives.

You will quickly realize my military background has shaped many of my core values and beliefs. Do not mistake this book as a treatise on military leadership. Accept that the military is an organization that quite literally lives and dies on the quality and performance of their leaders and spends significant time, money and effort to develop, nurture and promote the best and the brightest so they can excel in the most arduous of circumstances under combat conditions. One bad example of leadership you see in movies and on TV is when a boss says 'That is an Order'. I do not recall of ever having said that and believe that anyone that does has fundamentally failed as a leader. When you have to remind someone who the boss is, you are demonstrating significant weakness as the leader and need to start rethinking about your role going forward.

What follows are my top 10 principles of leadership that are really the core of who I am, how I think and how I strive to live my life. Following these 10 beliefs I offer a short comparison between leadership and management and then finish off this first section with a simplified approach to decision making.

Principle #1 - Leadership Must Be Visible

Leaders have to do more than sit on their proverbial thrones and pontificate. Leaders have to make the effort to be present and visible, not just to the people that directly report to them but also to all the people who are in their hierarchy or chain of command, even if many layers below them. This becomes quite a challenge when an organization is geographically dispersed, but that cannot be an excuse for not making the effort. Much will depend on the size of the organization and number of people at any given location and the relative level of the boss. As a general rule of thumb, the intent of the visits or open meetings should be to reinforce the organizational vision, mission and key objectives or goals. As well, they can be used to get feedback on how well these and other key messaging is being passed and implemented through the organization. Through simple chats with subordinates as you do a walk around, you can determine if policy updates or changes are being effectively communicated, learn firsthand how people are feeling about the organization and their jobs and whether there may be different or improved ways to doing things that might reduce costs, create efficiencies and the like.

When leaders do their visits and walk-abouts they do have to be sensitive to possible issues they can inadvertently create. First and foremost, they should be aware that they could be meeting and talking with people that may not be part of their extended team so they have to be careful about giving explicit direction. They also have to be mindful of who is not present, especially subordinate leaders and managers, whose people are present. It is not uncommon for junior members to sound off on issues and policies and their bosses and the leader should not react in the moment but rather take all this in and make sure all 'sides' are reviewed and understood before any action is taken.

Over the past few years, town hall type meetings have become quite popular and they tend to be a combination of briefings or presentations or updates followed by a question and answer session. Whereas most of the meeting is organized and even scripted in many cases, the Q&A is usually a no-holds barred affair. Leaders must be very mindful about the impact of quick answers in these types of forums as they can have long term effects on the organization.

If decisions or actions are taken or committed to, it is very important these be properly communicated in a timely manner. It is incredibly frustrating to learn from one of your direct reports that your boss or someone even higher gave direction that you were completely unaware of, especially if it contradicted or countermanded something you had already put in motion. By communicating in a formal way that includes all necessary people, especially those who were not present when the decision was taken, it reduces potential misunderstandings or misinterpretations about what was actually said or decided.

By being present and visible, a leader does not only hear firsthand what people are thinking and experiencing but it is a significant opportunity to inspire and motivate. I distinctly remember when I was living in the Edmonton area as a Reserve Commander and a plane full of soldiers was returning from Afghanistan. It was customary that all the local Commanders would meet the plane at the airport to welcome home the troops before they were escorted through the City by the Edmonton Police to the Garrison where their families were gathered. On this plane were half a dozen wounded soldiers whose families were allowed to come to the airport as these soldiers were being transferred to local medical facilities. Just before the Airbus arrived, a Canadian Forces Challenger jet arrived with the Chief of the Defence Staff, General Rick Hillier and this was about 10 PM Edmonton time. I chatted with his Executive Assistant who told me they were leaving as soon as all the soldiers were on the buses because he had an 8 AM appointment with the Minister in Ottawa. General Hillier worked all day in Ottawa, flew four hours to Edmonton for about 90 minutes and flew four hours back to Ottawa just in time to meet the Minister so he could meet the families of the wounded and all the soldiers returning home; one of the best examples of Leadership being Visible I can remember.

Principle #2 - Lead By Example

Leading by example really comes down to the simple idea that you should not ask others to do something you have either not personally done or are prepared to do first. This is very easily understood in the military where officers are expected to lead from the front but what about the corporate or business world? I apply the concept of Do, Show, Coach to make the point that leadership is not about telling but rather about teaching and when necessary, correcting both actions and behaviors. My only caution is for senior leaders not to get so entrenched in this concept that they actually start doing low level tasks best left to others; the suggestion here is not that leaders should avoid menial or manual labour but rather they should be sensitive that when they are doing those things, they are probably not managing the greater process or operation and might miss something relevant or important. It is a fine line that can only be handled in the moment.

Following on from the concept of Do, Show, Coach is the idea that leaders are really also great mentors to one or more of their subordinates. I came up with the adage a number of years ago that 'for every Mentor there is a Tormentor'; that is to say that the person you are mentoring should torment you with questions, ask for advice and sometimes drive you a bit nuts with some of the things they do as they learn and grow. As a leader and mentor, you need to be well prepared for this and demonstrate patience and understanding, all the while keeping the 'tormentor' on track with a firm hand where needed.

Double standards are where there are clearly defined policies or rules guiding actions or behaviours but a lack of leadership allows certain individuals to operate outside the rules without repercussions or consequences. The absolute worst way of leading by example is when the leader is the one who flaunts or breaks the rules. Remember that you can lead by good or bad example and like news, the bad examples will spread so much more quickly than any number of good examples.

14

On the flip side, I am a strong believer in the concept of 'Rank Has Its Privilege'. Leadership is not about democracy where everyone has a vote and every vote counts equally and therefore everyone regardless of rank or title should be treated exactly the same. Leaders in all organizations are accorded privileges, whether it is the corner office or cubicle by the window, special parking spot or business class travel. However, it should be clear that these are typically well defined and are really like additional benefits other than pay that are extended with promotions or appointments. The bad leadership example occurs when leaders abuse their positions, ignore the guidelines and give themselves or select personnel special treatment.

Do not confuse proficiency or expertise in a specific task as a prerequisite for a leader. The best athlete on a team is often not the captain and the best salesman or engineer does not run the company. One of the best adages I ever heard was that 'the A students are working for the C students'! The best leaders understand what needs to be done and are able to marshal and motivate others to get the task done, and then acknowledges the efforts of those others both privately and publicly.

Remember the movie We Were Soldiers where Mel Gibson played the role of Lieutenant Colonel Hal Moore who was the Commanding Officer of an infantry battalion fighting in the Vietnam War? Based on the book We Were Soldiers Once by retired Lieutenant General Hal Moore and author Joe Galloway who was also present at the battle, the movie does a tremendous job of demonstrating superb Leadership by Example in both Hal Moore played by Mel Gibson and his Sergeant Major Basil Plumley played by Sam Elliot. I highly recommend reading the book and watching the movie, not just for the entertainment value but to see and understand the quality of the leadership displayed.

Principle #3 - Leaders Must Know What It Like To Be Led

One of the earliest lessons I learned about leadership is that 'before you lead, you must first know what it is like to be led'. This is a fundamental principle of military leadership training where everyone starts at the same level and someone from your peer group holds a temporary appointment as the 'leader'. It changes regularly, so for one task or day or week you could be the boss only to find yourself as a follower next time around. The better you are at taking direction, the better you should be at giving it, as you will have a core understanding of what it is like on both sides of the equation.

For a very long time in the corporate and business world this same philosophy existed as most people started out in entry level positions including the mail room. Over time and with experience, they were promoted to the point where very many became very senior Managers and Executives. In the process they knew everything about how the organization operated and what it was like in a large number of departments and specific jobs. Today we see hordes of graduates joining companies with incredible academic credentials from Masters degrees to Business School certificates that start in junior leadership roles without ever spending any real time in the day to day of what the company does. This is well exemplified on reality TV where many of the CEOs who go 'undercover' have never even visited parts of the company they go to work in, let alone have any real appreciation for what their working people do any given day.

Of particular concern is the leadership situation of small and medium sized businesses which are very often family oriented or owner driven. What starts out as a modest effort grows over time into a fairly significant operation. With limited, if any, defined Human Resources staff there are seldom formal leadership development programs. It really comes down to luck or circumstances that there is any effective leadership at all. These privately held companies are not under the same scrutiny of a public company with an independent board, tighter accounting rules and the like. Having been in this situation a couple times, there is little regard or interest for personal development training simply because it costs money and every dollar spent is effectively coming out of the owner's pocket.

This leads to the long debated issue of whether leaders are born or developed, with or without formal training. Like everything else when it comes to people, there is no question there are many who display an innate sense or ability to lead much like others have superb athletic skills or are predisposed to be teachers or care givers. However, just like great athletes require outstanding coaching and progressively more challenging levels of competition and doctors require years of formal education and experience, the best leaders are those who have been trained, coached and mentored through various positions and appointments. There are always exceptions where, with little to no training or experience, someone will rise up as a leader, however this really is the exception.

Principle #4 - Are You Decisive Or Impulsive?

A good or great leader knows how to make good or great decisions and as importantly knows how to implement or execute the decisions of his or her superiors. However, just because you make good decisions does not mean you are a leader; each and every day you make dozens and dozens of decisions about what to wear, where to eat, etcetera that have no effect on anyone else. It is only the decisions that affect others that determine if you are or are not a leader and the quality of those decisions is what, in part, defines how good a leader you are.

When faced with a decision do you act or react? Do you step through a decision process or do you simply allow instinct or intuition to guide you? The first thing you have to identify is how long do you have to make the decision and take action, as this will likely be the key factor that determines how you will arrive at your decision. Where time is not a real issue you can do research, seek the advice and input of others and even do some testing of options to assist you with your final course of action. When time is short you may have to rely on knowledge, experience and your gut to guide you.

No matter how much you want to make your decision based on all the information, the reality is that you will often be forced to decide with incomplete or conflicting information. Sometimes waiting for more or better information is a good thing but in the end you have to make the decision or allow the circumstances absent of a decision to continue. Where time and circumstances allow, you should seek the advice of others. It is not a good idea to ask your boss for advice; once he or she has given their opinion or advice you are hard pressed to not follow it, especially if the ultimate outcome is not what was desired or expected. Instead, gather your group of trusted advisors that might include peers or subordinates and engage with them to harness ideas and options. Allow rigorous debate, encourage contrarian perspectives and examine all courses open but in the end it does come down to the leader to make the final decision.

18

A couple of cautionary notes about collaborative decision making. After over eight years of experience either in formal training or operational units, I was transferred to a staff position at headquarters in Ottawa. It seemed all we did was sit in meeting after meeting of organized committees, where I was never sure if anything was ever accomplished. After one particularly frustrating day I commented 'decisions by committee absolve individuals of responsibility' only to have a very senior officer retort 'decisions by committee disappear'. The message here is it is okay to seek the advice and recommendations of others but the leader alone must make the decision. More importantly, the leader must accept total responsibility for the outcome of the decision.

The second note is directed to those who have the opportunity to participate in the decision making collaboration. If you have insight or information that is germane or relevant to the matter at hand, you are ethically bound to offer it. If you disagree with the pending decision and are given the chance to express your concerns and views ahead of the final decision you have an obligation to do so in a respectful and professional manner. Once the decision has been made you really must support it as if it was your decision, for to do anything but would be both disingenuous and could potentially appear disloyal.

Principle #5 - Be Irrelevant And Not Irreverent To Your Success

Another key principle of leadership I completely subscribe to is the philosophy that you can only really get to the top by being held up on the shoulders of others. In the military we were assessed on how well we had prepared our subordinates to do our jobs. To test this, especially during training exercises, we were arbitrarily 'injured or killed' and forced to watch to see how well one of our subordinates was prepared to step up and replace us.

In all my years in the traditional business world I have never once seen this; most bosses are borderline paranoid that if they develop a subordinate to be able to do their job, they may not be needed anymore. Many companies and organizations have structured leadership and mentorship programs to identify and develop the next generation of rising stars, however it is often up to the direct supervisor to provide that final bit of coaching and guidance that makes a real difference. Unfortunately, much of the time, that is missing. Also often ignored or misunderstood is that the direct supervisor is responsible for either formal or informal performance reports and they can very easily torpedo the career of rising stars they do not like or support or feel threatened by.

You would expect that, as a matter of course, senior executives would actively seek out and promote people who clearly demonstrate an ability to develop leadership and management skills in others but even doing that is a learned skill. Often in conflict with this are bureaucratic driven policies or union contracts, where seniority trumps all else and eventually an organization ends up with a leadership cadre that exemplifies what is commonly referred to as the Peter Principle. This is where people have risen to a level of incompetence after being promoted and rewarded for service and competence at a lower level without demonstrating any ability or aptitude to actually succeed at the higher position. As counterintuitive as this may sound, it is highly prevalent in government and business. It is sort of like the astronaut that said something to the effect that his greatest worry was the spaceship he was riding was a collection of parts and systems all built by the lowest priced supplier and contractors! It takes very strong, dedicated and special leaders to overcome the inertia of these entrenched issues. Very often they have to have come from outside the organization with a mandate and authority to effect change to have any real lasting impact.

Two industries that do support this are Network Marketing and Direct Sales where everyone is an independent contractor whose growth and income potential in the 'program' is directly linked to their ability to develop other leaders. The really successful companies from these industries have a long track record of providing outstanding training and mentorship opportunities for those who choose to take of advantage of what is offered.

Closely linked to this is the idea that 'knowledge is power' where some believe that by keeping information to themselves they become power brokers to protect or advance their own interests, even if at the expense of the company. My most vivid example of this came from a close friend who at one point in his career had joined a company in a senior manager role. After a few months, he recognized that by spending a few hundred thousand dollars he could improve productivity and increase profits significantly. What he did not know and had never been briefed on was that his boss and the President had briefed the Board on a plan to spend more than 10 times the amount to gain about the same net benefit. Not only was his plan outright rejected but he was fired without the Board ever being made aware of his plan. Rather than presenting my friend's plan as a viable alternative and in the process showing he had been a great hire with outstanding potential, he was let go for being a threat. Knowledge is not power; it is only through acting on knowledge that power can be created.

Principle #6 - The 3 Legged Stool Of Leadership

The big three are responsibility, authority and accountability. They are inseparable and yet it never surprises me when I see them being treated as distinct and separate with little to no connectivity. Our society seems to have developed the perspective or attitude that as soon as something goes wrong in an organization, the person at the top should be held to account. I completely disagree with this view unless it can be shown he or she had either created a culture that allowed the mistake to happen or he or she had not properly delegated. I am also somewhat concerned that there is a general atmosphere of 'personal responsibility avoidance' that has developed in our society that not just condones but encourages individuals to point the finger everywhere except at themselves.

Leaders who do not delegate are not leaders. Delegating is an art form that requires practise and some measure of experience. The mistake most often made is to delegate responsibility and accountability without the commensurate authority to actually deliver on the delegated task. In effect, what this does is handcuff the subordinate and force him or her to come back to the boss to make or enforce decisions. This can be especially disempowering when the delegated task requires peer level cross functional or departmental collaboration and coordination and where something like getting all the right people to a meeting can be challenging. In a perfect world, the boss would give the subordinate the equivalent of their own authority, but in practise this seldom happens. At a minimum, the boss must stand behind the subordinate in all decisions; the best way to avoid issues or conflicts is to clearly define at the outset what the boundaries are and under what circumstances or situations the subordinate must brief the boss in advance of a decision being taken. The kiss of death in a delegated authority situation is when the boss overrules the subordinate after the fact; the subordinate no longer has any moral authority to continue in that specific role or task and ultimately must be replaced.

Perhaps most dangerous is authority without accountability. When someone has the ability to give direction or act without having to face the consequences of their actions, an organization is significantly imperilled and unfortunately this is far more prevalent than most people realize. Look closely at your own work circumstances and I am sure you can find a couple of situations where promotions have been gifted and not earned; a family member in the business whose actions or behaviors are accommodated, or a long serving employee whose loyalty is used as an excuse to ignore performance issues.

Perhaps the greatest challenge of leadership may well be when there is no explicit or defined authority. In most organizations the person with the most rank has the most authority and can impose their will and decisions on others. What about where there is no obvious leader or where the leader has no specific authority; the 'you can't tell me what to do' attitude is alive and well and it can be a significant test of leadership to get things done in this environment. Think of volunteer organizations, community groups, trade associations or even teams of independent contractors like network marketers, many real estate and insurance agents and the like. In order to lead in groups like this, there is much more collaboration and consensus building and often the leader stands out as one who is willing to invest the time and energy for the betterment of the organization.

Principle #7 - Business Not Personal

How often have both bosses and subordinates become confused or conflicted because a personal relationship has gotten in the way of getting on with business? You have all heard adages like 'strictly business, nothing personal but' or 'it is lonely at the top' or 'leadership is not a popularity contest'. They are all true but what is challenging is understanding how to work with these complex relationships. It can be especially difficult when two or more people have spent years together in an organization where, for the most part they were peers, only to find themselves now in a situation where one has been promoted ahead of them and now is their direct or superior boss.

There is another adage that says 'familiarity breeds contempt' but in my view this only occurs when there is weak or ineffective leadership. As long as everyone knows who the boss is and there is mutual respect both up and down this should never be an issue. However, there will still be potential for the lines to be a bit gray or sometimes you just need to reset the bar and ensure there is no confusion. The best technique I have used for this is to take a clean piece of paper and draw a line down the middle from top to bottom. On the left hand side print in big letters BUSINESS and on the right hand side PERSONAL. Many years ago I was in business with my Father and we needed to have this kind of discussion and I agonized for days until I figured out this approach. I said to him "we are father and son and we have a great personal relationship but for now we are on the BUSINESS side of the page." By setting the stage in that manner, we were able to have a very good meeting and resolved most of what was causing grief. At the end, once we had agreed to our go-forward plan, I finished the session with "give me a hug and let's get a beer." No egos, no unnecessary emotional baggage, just open and honest communication to work through one or many issues.

Do not confuse friendship and respect. In the best of situations, you will both like and respect your boss and hope the same holds true for your subordinates but this is not always the case. Obviously, the worst case scenario is when you neither like nor respect your boss and that can really only lead to significant work challenges that usually ends badly for someone. What is quite common is when you do not particularly like your boss and probably only socialize as necessary and yet you really respect him or her professionally. As long as you maintain a cordial working relationship where you both understand the business versus personal construct, this can be very effective model for success. I call this the 'roast beef effect' where I would follow a leader over the proverbial hill but I would not invite them to a roast beef dinner at my home. Over the years I have had a number of these relationships that worked very well as there was no conflict or confusion about who was in charge.

Principle #8 - Leading Leaders Versus Leading Followers

Oddly enough, most leaders either do not understand or appreciate how much different it is to lead followers than it is to lead other leaders. In fact, I would go so far as to say it is the latter that is the root of most organizational dysfunction today. The idea that one size fits all when it comes to leadership is completely wrong. A very simple way to make sure you stay on track is to remember One Down and Two Up.

If you think of a typical organizational chart it shows a series of layers or levels to indicate who reports to whom. One Down means you only give direction or orders or tasks to those people who directly report to you. This also means you should only get direction from the person you report to. Two Up teaches that it is important to understand contextually what the person two above you is trying to accomplish; what is their intent? Knowing and understanding the direction you have been given allows you to frame your decisions in line with your superior bosses overall intent. Also guiding you will be organizational mandates like the mission and vision statements which can also come into play when you need to make a decision.

Leading other leaders very much changes the dynamic of how you interact with them. The main difference is there should be more potential for collaboration and consensus before a decision is taken and the more senior and experienced the leaders, the more this is expected. Followers neither expect nor deserve the same degree of 'consultation'; in most cases they just want clear unambiguous direction. Having said all this, all good leaders know that in exigent circumstances there may be no time for collaboration and direction must be passed and acted upon quickly, often through multiple layers of leadership and in the process it cannot be altered or changed. Think about the discipline required to keep the full letter and intent of direction intact through multiple layers; remember the fireside game of passing a story around the circle and laughing at how mangled the final version became after only 4 or 5 iterations!

Principle #9 - Leadership Is Not An 8-5 Job

As leadership is really all about people, it has to be accepted that it is a 24 hour a day responsibility. Too many junior leaders in particular think there is an ON/OFF switch; when it is ON they are in charge with all the associated duties and when it is OFF they are just 'one of the boys', so to speak. The harsh reality is it is never off and how you conduct yourself outside the formal work environment is just as important as when you are at work or on duty. That does not mean you cannot relax or even socialize with subordinates who may also be friends or family, rather it simply requires you to be aware that you are the leader and act accordingly.

One other aspect of this is that the leader must be respectful of the clock and the demands and expectations of their subordinates. I have too many personal examples of meetings being called at the end of the day that cut into what should be personal time to deal with issues that could easily wait until the next day or next week. I have never figured out if the boss is simply asserting their authority or simply ignorant of the time and knock-on effects of doing this with frequency.

Principle #10 - Share Success And Accept Blame

Have you heard the adage that 'people will do more for recognition than for money'? Many will scoff at this notion and yet, think back to the last time someone you really respected said "thank you for your effort today because you really made a difference"; how did that make you feel? Then think about the last time you opened your pay check; how did that make you feel? Most people get tremendous satisfaction when their contributions are acknowledged, especially when it is done well and in front of other coworkers.

Good leaders not only understand this, they take full advantage of it whenever possible. Like all tools, if recognition is overused it loses value but when strategically managed and judiciously levered, it can be a powerful morale and loyalty multiplier. Recognition programs do not have to include extra bonus money or rewards like trips or gifts. They can simply be ad hoc or in the moment thank you speeches or more formal presentations with certificates for long service, a job well done, etcetera. When or if leaders receive recognition for what they have accomplished, it costs nothing to ensure this recognition is passed down into the team or organization that worked with and supported the leader.

Blame, however, is an entirely different matter. A strong leader will ascribe to the notion of 'the buck stops here', which is to say the leader will accept the responsibility and associated blame when it was their decision or actions that created the issue in the first place. If the leader has properly and effectively delegated the authority, responsibility and accountability to a subordinate who was also well prepared and coached to be successful but still caused or did not prevent the issue, then the leader should not take the fall for that person.

Leadership Versus Management

I am not sure why but for some strange reason far too many people believe Leadership and Management are fundamentally the same and in my view this is completely wrong. Good leaders can be good managers and vice versa but this is most often not the case. Rather than get into a long winded debate over definitions, I am going to contrast and compare leaders and managers by looking at 5 examples to highlight my perspective and show key differences. Many who read this will suggest it is all about semantics, however I ask that you not pass judgement until after you have read and reflected on these against personal experiences.

Example #1 - Managers React And Leaders Act

Remember my personal adage that Management is the Science of Reaction and Leadership is the Art of Action. I am personally convinced that this one distinction is a key differentiator between Managers and Leaders. This does not mean that Leaders will always take action in advance of a situation. Rather, it suggests that Leaders will work through a disciplined decision process, and with purpose and intent respond to the situation. They know full well they may need to stay engaged to monitor and, if necessary, provide further direction or guidance as appropriate. As an example, you have 6 people who report to you and one of them resigns with no warning. A manager would probably immediately start the process to fill the position or if under budget pressure maybe simply decide to leave it vacant. A leader would probably do multiple things including try to find out the real reason for the resignation, conduct a review to determine how critical the position is to figure out whether to fill it with a promotion or new hire or possibly leave vacant if appropriate. To many these may seem like the same thing but philosophically they are very different.

Example #2 - You Manage Resources – You Lead Individuals

You can manage an individual's schedule, you can manage their career, you can manage their performance but you must lead the individual. When you start down the path of managing the individual you lose perspective on the skills, abilities, strengths and weaknesses that make the individual unique amongst others. Leadership is highly personal whereas Management is very impersonal. Nowhere is this more obvious than when large organizations downsize and little or no attention is paid to the individual and decisions are taken based purely on numbers or seniority.

Example #3 - Managers Focus On Rules – Leaders Focus On Values

Any organization that puts Rules ahead of Values limits its potential for success. Rules are important but secondary to clearly articulated and well understood Values. Rules are not always well defined; some are written down but many are more cultural based on what has been allowed or approved in the past. By default, if your first step to resolving a problem or issue is to look to the Rules then you are in Management mode. This is not a criticism but rather a reality. Another way of stating this is the adage that 'Managers do Things Right whereas Leaders do the Right Things'[1]. This does not mean that Leaders can flaunt the rules and simply do what they want; rather it suggests that Leaders should not ever be compelled to blindly follow rules without understanding the full context of the situation and circumstances.

As a simple example let's say the Rule is that nobody below the level of Vice President can authorize flying business class and anyone who does will be required to pay back the difference in cost and receive verbal counselling. You are a Director that reports to a VP and you have a member of your team that just submitted an expense report with a business class airfare without any VP authorization, so what do you do? If you follow the Rule you will approve the expenses but disallow the $400 extra for business class and you will have to schedule a verbal counselling session with your team member. Instead you call in the person to ask why they upgraded and learned the onsite work had extended the trip by one day. The only option to getting home was to fly business class that day or wait until the next day which offset the $400 upgrade fee by approximately $250 for additional hotel, car and meals. Perhaps most importantly, the person's wife was scheduled for minor surgery the next day which had been booked for weeks and could not be easily changed. It was also pointed out that the person tried to call both you and the VP but both were unavailable and a decision had to be taken right away. Knowing that one of your Company core Values is to provide a work environment that respects and supports quality family life, it is should be a simple decision to allow the upgrade and brief the VP on the situation.

Example #4 - Managers Focus On Process, Leaders Focus On Outcomes

Process is important but only if it serves the organization and gets you to the desired result or outcome. When following the process becomes more important than achieving the outcome, you are in danger of becoming a slave to the process which is not a good thing. As well defined and understood a process is, there may be time or situations where an exception needs to be made for practical or expediency reasons. When completely avoiding the process becomes the rule rather than the exception, you have a culture crisis that goes well beyond process and outcome. A Manager will insist on process simply because that is how it is supposed to be and often it is their role in the process that gives them perceived influence or power they are typically unwilling to forego. A Leader will focus on the outcome supporting the process but continually looking for ways to improve or streamline the process if and when necessary.

Example #5 - Managers Insist On Compliance, Leaders Ask For Commitment

This is perhaps more philosophical than the others but it does highlight quite dramatically the mindset difference between Managers and Leaders. Compliance is all about following the rules and the processes, understanding and accepting your limits of authority, not accepting responsibility for anything you do not have to and most pointedly, where your success is measured by your lack of failure. Commitment is all about doing what you said you would do long after the emotion you said it with has left you. What Leaders do is, on an individual and collective basis, provide a vision and goals and ask for their reports to make the commitment to meet or exceed those expectations.

Section 1 Bonus – A Decision Making Process

There are countless references in libraries and on the web where you can go to learn about decision making strategies and processes but what follows will be an overview of a simple and easy to follow process that works well for both personal and business decisions. Further, rather than just providing an overview of the process and necessary steps, I will offer a comprehensive example to give real insight into the level of detail and complexity that may be necessary to make a good decision that can withstand the challenges of time and circumstances.

Step 1 – Set your Aim or Goal or Objective or Mission. Different words but all saying that you absolutely must make sure that you are very clear and completely unambiguous as to what your decision is supposed to accomplish. For complex challenges, you may need to complete a full analysis of what from now on will be called the Aim. Especially when the Aim is assigned by a boss it is critical you get this correct, otherwise you could go a long way down a path including committing resources only to find you are working on the wrong thing. As silly or absurd as this may sound, it is not really that uncommon.

For example, what if your boss sends you a quick note and asks you to 'create a plan to increase sales by 50 percent in Europe for presentation to the Executive Team next Friday morning'. Do you really believe you have all the information necessary to move ahead or do you have some very specific questions that need to be answered before you really get engaged? Perhaps your background and understanding of the issues and having worked for this boss for a while allow you to forge ahead. What if you need to get questions like 'by when?' or 'what budget increase for additional staff and travel is available?' or 'are new products or services being launched?' answered, just to name a few.

Another key part of the Aim is understanding what specific limitations there are to the Aim that are effectively imposed and must be worked with and catered to in your decision process. In the example above, you must be prepared to make a presentation to the Executive Team next Friday morning. For illustrative purposes you complete a simple Aim analysis and get answers to the three questions above as 'within the next fiscal year which starts in 60 days', 'make recommendations on staff and travel increases as part of your plan including budgetary estimates for consideration' and ' no new products or services beyond what is already on the roadmap'. Given these answers, the only other real imposed limitation to the Aim would be that the 50% sales increase must be achieved in the next fiscal year.

The last part of setting the Aim is to articulate what assumptions you are making. In this example, you might have a couple like 'the new products on the roadmap will be available for sale on time as currently planned' or 'exchange rates to the Euro and British Pound will remain the same for the next fiscal year'.

Having completed this first step and where time permits, it is not a bad idea to brief your boss and get his or her sign off before continuing. In many cases this may not be possible and in many cases you might be doing this for your own purposes, so there may be no one to discuss this with but where you can it is highly recommended. When you are the boss and you have delegated this process to someone, it is suggested you build this review step into the process just to ensure there is no confusion or false assumptions. As tedious and detailed as this might appear for simple problems and decisions, this is something you might do in your head in a matter of a couple of minutes, but for complex issues and especially for business, following a disciplined and documented process is a better way to proceed.

Step 2 – Influencers and Factors. This is the real meat of the process as it is in this step that you examine and analyse all the potential factors and influencers that must be taken into consideration as part of the decision making process. More importantly, you need to drill down and for each factor identified present one or more conclusions that flow from the factor. It is important to take particular time and effort to keep answering the question 'so what' until you cannot find any more answers. Continuing with our earlier example a few key factors and resulting conclusions might include

1. The European office is located in Frankfurt. SO WHAT?
   a. Frankfurt is centrally located in Europe with great road, rail and air access. SO WHAT?
      i. From a geographic perspective there is no requirement to look at changing the European office location.
2. Sales leadership for Europe is provided from the North American head office. SO WHAT?
   a. Time change differences significantly limit day to day involvement of Sales Leadership in the European business. SO WHAT?
      i. Create a European Sales Leader position in Frankfurt. SO WHAT?
         1. Either promote someone in European team or hire a new person or move someone from North America. SO WHAT?
         2. Do cost/benefit analysis for each option. ACTION ITEM!
   b. Limited ability for Sales Leader to directly work with, coach and mentor team. SO WHAT?
      i. Same as a. above
   c. Limited ability for Sales Leader to develop key customer relationships. SO WHAT?
      i. Same as a. and b. above
3. There is no warehousing in Europe. SO WHAT?
   a. Order fulfillment typically takes 2 weeks longer than in North America. SO WHAT?

      i.   Business is lost for short lead time orders. SO WHAT?

          1. Stock higher moving items in Frankfurt. SO WHAT?

          2. Confirm space for stocking is available. SO WHAT?

          3. Do cost/benefit analysis. ACTION ITEM!

     ii. Focus sales team on higher value projects where price and delivery are secondary to value-add and service. SO WHAT?

          1. Requires significant sales training and mentoring on an ongoing basis. SO WHAT?

              a. Require more Sales Leadership more often in Europe. ACTION ITEM.

4. European sales are based on a direct to customer sales model by a direct sales team of 5 each with multiple country responsibilities supported by an inside sales team of 2 in Europe and 3 in North America to provide quotes and other sales support. SO WHAT?

     a. Outside sales team is 'on the road' 60 percent of the time. SO WHAT?

     b. Time zone and travel issues impact inside sales support turnaround times. SO WHAT?

     c. Strengthen European based Inside Sales team. SO WHAT?

     d. Do cost benefit analysis on Inside Sales. ACTION ITEM and SO WHAT?

     e. More European Sales staff may require European Sales Leadership. ACTION ITEM!

5. Our primary two competitors in the European market are headquartered in Brussels and Barcelona and each have multiple offices in various European countries. SO WHAT? By now you should be getting a real sense of what it takes to complete this

analysis. The more detail you work through the more action items and conclusions you will end with.

Step 3 – Identify Courses or Options. There is a tendency in this step to try to have a long list of options, but realistically if the AIM is properly defined and constrained, there will probably be no fewer than two and no more than five. Avoid the trap of creating 'straw man' options that cannot stand up to any real review and are discarded early on, as this simply reduces the overall credibility of your effort. For each course of action, you need to do a Pro and Con or Advantages and Disadvantages analysis. This analysis should flow directly from the conclusions arrived at during the Influencers and Factors review based on the answers to the SO WHAT process. Introducing new conclusions at this stage not previously discussed only undermines the integrity of your work.

Step 4 – Recommendation and Plan. If you are doing this for yourself you should be making the decision. If you are doing this for a boss or committee you need to make a recommendation. You do not need to add a lot of justification to your recommendation as it should be quite obvious from your Options analysis. There will be circumstances where two or more options all may work and in this situation you may want to provide some specific reason for selecting or recommending one above the other(s).

Once you have made your decision or recommendation, the final part of the process is to prepare a draft plan for review and action. Many of the key headings and specifics of the plan will come directly from the detailed analysis so this is really more about organizing, compiling and scheduling tasks and activities than anything else.

Give this a try next time you have a complex decision or recommendation to make and see how it works for you then tweak or adjust it as necessary to fit your style and situation.

Section 2 – Sales Leadership Challenges

Background

You know the old adage 'if it was easy anyone could do it'. Sales Leadership and Management definitely are not easy and the harsh truth is they can be very difficult. The first thing you must do is understand what your role and responsibilities include. For example,

1. Do you carry a revenue target and have a primary responsibility to sell, in addition to your sales leadership duties?
2. Do you have HR responsibilities like hiring and firing?
3. Do you have subordinate sales leaders reporting to you?
4. Is your sales leadership team and/or your sales team dispersed geographically?
5. How much do you travel and how does that support or limit your ability to lead and manage?

The lifeblood of all business is revenue; bring it in and you can be immensely successful but the flip side is also true. What makes all sales jobs even more complicated is that your results are very often visible to a large part of the company. It can be hugely difficult to hide from a bad week, month or quarter, whereas lots of people in other jobs can go months without their performance being dramatically obvious to most others. Even minor customer facing mistakes can prove to be disastrous resulting in the loss of a sale or worse.

What I am going to do next is highlight and discuss 25 of the most significant challenges a Sales Leader might face in their current or any future position. Of course this list is not exhaustive but what is presented is based on personal experience in some form or fashion.

Challenge #1 – Everyone Believes They Can Sell!

Without a doubt, I am confident this is the number one challenge all Sales Leaders will encounter and usually sooner rather than later. The irony is that most of those who think or believe they can sell would never want any responsibility for selling, but they want to tell you how to do it better or how to better manage your sales team. Where this gets painful, is that if you ever try to make any suggestions on how their people might do something different or better, you will most likely get told to mind your own business, sometimes politely and sometimes not.

You need to anticipate this will happen and you must be prepared for how to respond to it when it does. I am not a big proponent of the 'one size fits all approach' instead preferring to adjust and adapt my response to the situation and circumstances. To set the stage let's look at 3 different scenarios and offer advice on how to proceed for each including,

1. The challenge comes informally from a colleague or friend who is in a department other than sales, something like "why is your team not getting any new orders – can't they close?"

As this is just an informal question you need to use this situation as an opportunity to put to rest any concern this individual has about the quality or work ethic of the Sales team. Remember if one is asking the question, others may be thinking it and they all chat together too. Highlight all the good things that are happening in Sales like the growth of the pipeline, the number of recent good meetings with customers and all new and follow up meetings on the schedule. If one or more of your team are in a bit of a slump or funk, be honest (without using names) that there is significant coaching and mentoring going on. What I recommend you not do is get defensive and simply brush aside the questioner as being uninformed and out of touch.

2. The challenge comes during a formal meeting of peers that is chaired by a person senior to you, something like "you guys

have it easy; take your customers golfing or to lunch and get the order so why are you not getting the orders?"

Once again you need to avoid being defensive. Given the audience is primarily your peer group you now have a great opportunity to educate without lecturing about how the process works. If it is anyone's perception that buying lunch or golf is all it takes to get an order they have a very simplistic view of buyers. One trick I like to use is to reverse the situation; ask the person who asked the question if they made their business or personal buying decisions on something like a freebie and see how they respond or react. Most good sales people do not use these freebies to get the order, rather they use it to thank customers for previous business and to have informal discussions about future opportunities. As well, remind them the value of spending quality time with customers in a relaxed environment with few distractions. By all means ensure you advise this group the steps you work through with your team on 'closing' and what efforts are being taken on a couple of specific opportunities to show plenty is being done to ensure the future revenue.

3. The challenge comes from one or a group of senior people who are frustrated with the revenue and say something like "just get the team doing more sales calls and it will fix the problem."

In this situation you need to ensure the perception of the senior person or group is not the reality of the organization. You need to be forthright without being defensive. You need to show you really are aware of the situation and in control of what is being done. Do not try to educate and do not lecture about Sales process. Senior people often ask these types of questions without all the facts and in most cases do not have the time or desire to hear the facts; rather what they want is to be heard and acknowledged and know someone takes responsibility for getting things fixed.

Looking at what is common to all scenarios, it is obvious that at the root of these questions or challenges is the fact that these and most others not in sales do not really appreciate how involved the sales process can be. They also typically do not realize how dependent the sales team are on other parts of the organization to deliver value to customers that will lead to revenue generation results. What this means is that you have a responsibility to constantly educate non-sales types on what it really takes to bring in an order. It starts with finding the right person to talk to through the whole process of developing a relationship and gaining trust to making one or many presentations, preparing and presenting a proposal to following up and closing. Exacerbating the problem are salespeople who parade around the office gloating over the big orders they have brought in and how tough their week was with all the lunch meetings, etcetera. This adds fuel to the notion that selling is really about schmoozing and socializing and not tough like engineering or accounting work. In addition to ensuring you use every opportunity to remind non sales people about how difficult real professional sales can be, you need to constantly remind your team to do the same and not highlight the lunches, hockey games or golfing.

When there are no orders coming in, it suggests there is a major overarching issue that may or may not be Sales related. It could be everything from product quality or delivery issues, problems with pricing strategies or significant company related issues affecting your credibility or confidence in the marketplace. In these circumstances, you have to be careful to ask good questions as many will get very defensive very quickly to jealously guard their turf and in most cases try to deflect the blame back on Sales. Having said that, you still must make sure these issues are not overlooked or swept aside.

When a specific territory or two are struggling to maintain historical average revenues, then as Sales Leader you have a responsibility to take a very close look at what has changed or what is different that is causing this drop in revenue. The age, experience and tenure of the salesperson in the Territory should have little or no impact on how you act but you must act or you are effectively 'approving' of what is happening. These coaching, mentoring or leadership moments or opportunities cannot be ignored.

Challenge #2 – Your Boss Used To Be A Sales Leader

This challenge can take two forms, with the first being your Boss is a senior Sales Leader to whom you report or you are the senior Sales Leader reporting to the President or other very senior executive who now has a much broader role than just sales. This type of problem is not unique in Sales and exists in all organizations and departments, so understanding that is a good place to start. If your results are the same or better than when your Boss was the Sales Leader, you really do not have too much to be concerned about; it is only if your team is underperforming that this can become a real challenge for you.

If you report to a more senior Sales Leader, the next question is who hired you? If you were hired by your Boss, you should have fewer short term issues to deal with as your Boss will want to prove that hiring you was a good decision. What is really important is to have a very clear and unambiguous job profile and description where your role and responsibilities are well articulated and with little room for confusion. What is also really critical is that you and your Boss fundamentally agree on what the strategic approach to selling should be within the organization; how it plays out tactically or on a day to day basis should be your decision.

The other thing you have to be aware of in this situation is that your Boss may have both good and bad relationships with some of what are now your direct reports and that can create situations. An example of this might be that one of your team has become good friends with your Boss and they socialize together outside of the office and even in the office they may chat over coffee or go to lunch together. If you are that naïve to believe that work related things including you are not being discussed, you need to shake your head. My recommendation in this type of situation is to not feel left out or marginalized by that relationship. If you believe that situation is impacting the morale or performance of either this one individual or the Sales team at large or your ability to do your job effectively, then you must have a serious and planned discussion with your Boss. Note I recommend discussing this with the Boss and not your direct report first. Let the results of that discussion guide you on if, when and how you take this to your salesperson.

I have also personally had the experience of twice having a President who used to be in sales during the start-up phase of the business. In both situations, the President had been away from sales for many years and in my opinion was somewhat out of touch with many of the changes that virtual 24 hour a day and 7 day a week digital connectivity has brought to selling. For example, the notion that you can make a single phone call and get an appointment is long gone. Even when you have a great relationship with a customer, you have to have a reason for them to give you some of their valuable time. It is not uncommon to be asked something like "I have 10 minutes now so what do you want to talk about?" I am personally a huge believer in face to face meetings when they are warranted and in Section 3 will offer a number of ideas on getting the appointment but the simple fact that this requires unique skills and abilities confirms that it is not quite as easy as most non salespeople think.

The other big one that is happening today is that while you are in the process of trying to introduce yourself and get the appointment, especially when it is someone you have never met with before, they are hitting your website in real time while on the phone. In many cases, the quality of the website can have an immediate and direct impact on whether you can get their time. When you send introductory emails you must operate on the assumption they have will check you out, including possibly looking you up on social media sites like LinkedIn, Facebook and others. Whether you like it or not there are very many people these days who will judge you based on your online presence even if they have never met you!

All of this to say that having a President that used to be in sales is just one of those realities you will have to deal with. The best advice I can offer is try to learn as quickly as possible what some of his or her fundamental philosophies and strategies are when it comes to selling and managing a sales team and then stick within those undefined boundaries. I was the first VP Sales for a public company and once a week the CEO ran a meeting with my Sales team to discuss what was going on. Not only that, it was all discussion based with no CRM and not even a tabulated spreadsheet or anything like that; just handwritten notes from the previous meeting. As our Sales team grew from 5 to over 20 strong, this meeting became very unwieldy and was losing sight of the objective of giving the CEO and CFO the big picture. To overcome this, I started my own meeting, implemented a structured approach to tracking opportunities and then reported overall to the CEO and CFO in the weekly Executive meeting. The CEO went along with this but what I failed to appreciate at the time was how he wanted to have that direct and personal ability to provide guidance and commentary to Sales. Even though he knew it was not his role or responsibility, it created friction between us that I had to sort out by inviting him to a full Sales team meeting once a month. To this day I am not sure it completely satisfied him but at the time it did seem to take a lot of the pressure off.

Challenge #3 – You Have Hiring But Not Firing Authority

When I inherited one Sales team, my Boss told me to go out to the field and evaluate the team and come back with recommendations on how to get things moving again after a couple years of relatively flat results. When I told him a couple months later I would like to replace the whole team on a managed basis, this was way more than what he was prepared to allow. I was not even able to replace the least effective person as a message to the rest to get onboard with the new strategies and programs being implemented. In effect, I had just learned that I had hiring authority but not firing authority, unless it was something quite grievous from a performance or attitude type perspective.

What makes this a very real challenge is the sales people that report to you and especially those that have been around a while probably know that you have limited authority. Given that, they pretty much do what they want and pick and choose what parts of your plan they will support. As Sales Leader this is a one way ticket to disaster; you are in a no win situation unless, and I stress unless, you are getting outstanding results and nobody other than you really cares about what is or is not being done.

To add to this perspective, imagine one sales guy that is having a fantastic year on track to double his numbers and the CEO actually says in an Executive Meeting something to the effect that "I don't care if he works from his cabin on the lake all summer when he is getting those kinds of results." Emotionally you might agree but pragmatically and logically you are dealing with a salesperson that will not follow any process, will not put anything in the CRM, steps around or over people to get things done his way and so on and so on. You have little to no leverage to bring him back into line, not simply to show who the Boss is or to micromanage, but because you know that when things do start to flatten or go south this will become important again. To finish the lesson, it was barely a year later when things had gone south quite badly for this person that the CEO was demanding to know "what is this guy doing all day?"

I am not sure there is a solution but what I encourage you to do is reread the 3 Legged Stool of Leadership in Section 1 and then sit down and have a real meaningful discussion with your Boss about balancing your authority to match your accountability and responsibility. In the end if you are unable to do this, you will simply have to put up with no praise when things are going well and a lot of flak when results are poor.

Challenge #4 – Some Of Your Sales Team Are Protected Or Untouchable

This is sort of an extension to the last challenge but what makes it different is how you find out the limits you have and how you deal with it. We all like to think we have a 'Godfather' or 'Guardian Angel' looking out for us from a career point of view but that is not always the case. Many times you do have a mentor that offers guidance and advice and has your back when needed. In some circumstances, a more senior person in your company that has taken a liking to you will vouch for you or push to promote you and you may not even be aware of it. In many cases, they may not even be part of your 'chain of command' but perhaps you solved a problem for them or someone in their team and they are just in payback mode. The message here is that if you have or hope you have someone looking after you, then you should expect the same is happening with your team, especially if they joined the company before you. Over time you will figure out who is protected and by whom but you should use your peer network to learn if any of these relationships exist that might be hidden landmines for you later.

Other than finding out in advance, there are really only two ways you will learn of these situations. The first and simplest to deal with is when you make a comment about needing to either discipline or counsel someone on your team in a closed meeting with your Boss that might or might not include your peers and one of them says something like "I think he is one of your best guys so you might want to go easy on him." At least in this environment you can address it directly with open and probing questions why he or she makes that comment or suggestion. You can even pointedly challenge their point of view and take some measure of control. You can even go so far, if there is a group, to ask if anyone else has an opinion or wants to weigh in on this matter; in doing this you will definitely learn who sits where. Now just because someone disagrees with you on a personnel matter does not mean they are trying to protect the individual in question as they may be more concerned about the overall effect any disciplinary or other action may have on the organization at large.

The second way you find out is when someone else brings up the matter about this individual, normally in a private setting but sometimes in a manager or leader meeting. If your team member's performance problems are common knowledge, it could just be a normal question like "have you got a plan of how you are going to deal with this person?" If, however, the question is raised after you have had what you thought was a private counselling session with your direct report, then it is pretty obvious your person has gone around and talked to one or more people. Whether the person raising the issue is senior to you or not should not deter you from figuring out as quickly as possible just how far they might go to protect your direct report. It really is an opportunity for you to stake your ground and reinforce the fundamental principle that this is your responsibility and decision to take!

If you have a structured Human Resources department, I would recommend you discuss this with the right person in that team to get their opinion and insight on the situation. I also recommend you keep very good notes of what discussions were had on this issue in case it blows up in your face later. I do not believe in the concept of writing things down to 'cover your butt' but I do subscribe to keeping records simply because memories fade quickly and you do not want this to come to a hearsay or 'he said she said' situation that is not defensible should it become really messy.

It is important you know if any of your direct reports are protected and by whom because it can definitely change the dynamic of how you handle issues both with your direct report but also with the protecting person, especially if the protecting person is your Boss or higher up your reporting line. This is never a comfortable thing to have to deal with but it is a very real part of any workplace environment.

Challenge #5 –Making The Inside Sale

When you first start as Sales Leader there will be a honeymoon period where everyone seems to go out of their way to help you be successful. That will only last for a short time and you need to ensure that in that initial period, you set the stage with the rest of the company for long term support and assistance. It is well understood that in order for the company to be successful and bonuses to flow, the Sales team must first be successful at delivering revenue, but it does not necessarily follow that you and your team will always get moved to the front of the line when dealing with other departments. Remember everyone has their own responsibilities against which they are being constantly evaluated and sometimes what is important to you may not even appear on their priority list.

Many Sales Leaders I know believe that all they really need to do is have a great working relationship with their peer group and all will be fine. What this fails to recognize is that, just as you probably have some challenges with members of your team who do not always agree with you and adopt your priorities, it is quite likely the same holds true for your peers within their teams. It is up to you to make sure you develop your own direct relationships with as many of the people in the company as you can. It is really the little things that matter here; taking a moment to chat with others and expressing genuine interest in what they do and how they do it, acknowledging their efforts especially when they do something for you or your team and overall treating them with respect in every instance. I also recommend you follow the approach that you can always praise or thank staff in other departments for their work but you should never criticize or chastise them. If you have an issue, take it up with their supervisor.

Just having strong relationships and even alliances with people throughout the company will not be enough. As it is with outside customers, the relationship gives you the opportunity to be heard, so leverage that at every chance. Remember that not every sales opportunity will be priority one requiring special attention and you can only go to the proverbial well so often before you wear out your message. Additionally, expect your team is doing the same thing and make sure you and they are on the same page and not in competition for internal support and resources.

One example of just how important this can be is that you have received an order from a customer with a request to put a rush on it. There are no issues with the order, the underlying input costs are all correct and you have the necessary product in inventory so it sounds like a no-brainer. Unfortunately, the person who actually enters the order to trigger all the other internal actions has been having a bad day and has a backlog of work. Then your salesperson hand carries the order to their desk and insists it be taken care of immediately as a demand and not a request. What do you think is going to happen? It is quite likely that order gets set aside the minute the salesperson walks away or worse, the order entry person tells the salesperson to pound salt which just kicks up more dust and frustration. What started out as something very simple might now be a major internal crisis requiring multiple managerial interventions, all because someone failed to recognize that, just as you cannot demand an order from a customer, you cannot demand someone drop everything to work on your priority. By the way, that kind of situation created by your salesperson is another leadership opportunity for you.

The best way I have found to create widespread support is to be open and honest about the pipeline and in particular what is happening in the short term that may require additional time and effort. When every transaction, whether it is a quote or proposal or order, has always got to be done today, you will very quickly lose both credibility and support. Work hard with your team to understand the priorities and issues and then share that information broadly. Where staff from other departments do not seem to understand the strategic importance of an account or order, take the time to educate and not lecture and then ask for their support rather than demanding it. Just like customers where you have to continually make the sale, be prepared for this internally as well. It is as vital a part of what you do and manage on behalf of your Sales team as anything else.

Challenge #6 – Dealing With Multiple Offices And Staff

Things are so much simpler if everyone in the company works from one location. Throw in multiple offices in multiple time zones and it gets more complicated. Throw in multiple international locations where language could now be an issue and it can be incredibly challenging. Try to do all this over email and watch the fireworks in the distant sky!

As the Sales Leader, you should have both the mandate and ability to get out to the field and work with your team and that means travel. If and when you do visit remote offices, you need to ensure you take the time to do all the face to face personal things with as many of the staff as possible, even when they are not part of your direct team. It is much easier to work with people over phone and email once you have met them at least once. If your company offers video interacting, whether it is as simple as Skype or as complex as telepresence rooms, I recommend you take advantage of that wherever possible. One thing many are all guilty of when they are on the phone is pretending they are capable of multitasking; while they are believing they are giving the other party their full and undivided attention, they often find themselves reading email, looking stuff up online, etcetera. It is even worse when they are on multiple party conference calls and they can mute our microphone. Try this on a video link and it is pretty obvious.

One suggestion is to be sensitive to local times. Sending an email that arrives in their inbox very late in their day or after 'normal' work hours can create a lot of stress. You may be asking a simple question that can wait till tomorrow but how it is worded can create urgency that results in someone ruining a family outing to get back to you right away when it was not necessary. When sending something to multiple people in multiple time zones be sure to be clear about what you expect in response and by when. If you have members of your team that play a support role to the outside sales team, you may need to put in place flexible working hours to provide better overlap and create more hours of synergy and collaboration in real time.

The other issue you have to be aware of is what remote sales people are doing to meet their daily obligations, especially when there is no local direct supervisor or they work from a home office. I have both worked from home and managed many direct reports who worked from home. The typical response is to let the results speak for themselves, so when they are hitting or exceeding targets nobody really cares if they are putting in the hours. Be careful though; the instant the results start to slip watch for the comments to begin about everything from work ethic to professionalism.

What about the lone salesperson who has an office in a remote location? When he or she is in and out constantly and sometimes not even in for a day or two at a time, whispers begin from others about how they are not even working, even though you know they are very busy meeting customers and getting great results. The only way to avoid issues like this developing is to make sure your team is properly reporting their activities and you are effectively reporting to the organizations that Sales is giving it one hundred and ten percent each and every day.

Challenge #7 – Dealing With The Purchase Order Prevention Department

One of my guys was convinced the company had a PO Prevention Department. A salesperson receives a good order and shouts out "woo hoo – I got the order." Many in the rest of the company respond with "oh crap – he got the order"! What makes the PO Prevention Department really unique is that it is not an organized group with a manager and subordinates but more of an ad hoc coalition from all departments, who seemingly rally against the project or proposal both before and after the order is received in spite of this being core business. Reasons for their reluctance to support this business are many and varied. They do not like the salesperson, they do not believe they or their group have the capacity to do their part in winning or delivering, they think it is too risky especially for them or they just have the type of attitude that everything is based on the philosophies of NO or DON'T.

Just like it takes a village to raise a child, it takes a team to deliver to a customer. The more complex the order, the more departmental interdependencies there could be. For a simple order filled out of in-stock inventory it might only involve receiving the order, entering the order and filling and shipping the order. On the other extreme it could be a very involved technical solution where product management, engineering, operations, manufacturing and others all have a key role. If even one of them slips up, it could cause significant issues for the customer and the ultimate revenue stream.

The worst case scenario is when sales has received a PO for a complex solution and there is no clear record of how the solution was designed and quoted. You now have the challenge of having to accept the order and deliver, or reject the order and deal with all the incumbent issues that flow from that decision. For those of you that suggest this can never happen, I congratulate you for doing such a good job of burying your head in the sand. Every company gets so called 'bluebird' orders that are both non-forecast and unexpected. The greater issue is when a salesperson ignores the process and on their own generates a solution and quote and wins the business and then demands the company steps up and delivers. To me the bluebird situation is a management issue and the lone wolf salesperson is a leadership issue.

For a Sales Leader this is where it can get tricky. Many sales people are reluctant to provide too much visibility on what they are working on for a few reasons. For very large possible orders, they do not want to be constantly harassed (their perspective) for updates and questions like "where is the order?"; just review Challenge #1 again. For small pending orders, they just cannot be bothered with the time and effort to report them informally in conversations or formally in the CRM. In many cases, getting a credible forecast out of a customer is next to impossible and so you end up trying to manage things transactionally.

No question the best way to prevent the situation from becoming the rule rather than the exception is to have well defined and aggressively managed processes. A word on process; it only works if is serves the organization and not if the organization is turning inside out trying to serve the process. The most critical process to have to avoid running headfirst into the PO Prevention Department is the Sales and Quoting Process, that ties into whatever Customer Relationship Manager (CRM) you are using. For technical or complex quotes and proposals, your process should include visibility with input and/or review by all the departments before the quote or proposal is issued. This way, when the PO or contract arrives it is neither a surprise nor an opportunity for anyone to say something like "I or we did not agree to that." Going one step further I recommend that as the Sales Leader, you have a mandate and obligation to keep the organization well briefed on what is coming in terms of business. If there is ever a conflict over priorities they should be discussed and decided upon before the quote or proposal is issued and definitely before the order arrives. What does not work very well is the 'let's deal with that when we get the order' attitude, as that is simply procrastination or what I like to call business suicide on the installment plan.

Challenge #8 – Creating And Managing The Forecast

The forecast, the funnel and the pipeline are all terms for the same thing; the future revenue the company depends on to survive and grow. As Sales Leader you must own the forecast and each member of your Sales team must accept that they, in turn, own their own portion of it as well. It must be accurate and it must be kept current and no excuses should be accepted if either is not in place. Easy to say but really tough to execute. A quick internet search revealed at least three books available on this subject alone. As well, many of your customers will steadfastly either refuse to provide you a forecast or if they do, it is not typically worth relying much on. It really does come down to how well your team are able to build the forecast for each account.

First of all, maintaining a good forecast really depends on having a good Customer Relationship Manager (CRM) in place. Next, you have to make sure your team actually uses the CRM. If they are expected to spend most of their time out of the office meeting customers, when do they do their CRM updates? Does your CRM offer a mobility based app that runs on your designated smartphones? If so, can you really use it to enter much information or is just a way for them to access information on the fly? Have you put in place simple processes and forms that make data entry and updating easy and not too time consuming? Perhaps most importantly, have you overcome the first key objection sales teams have for CRMs, namely that it is corporate only tool that offers nothing of value back to the sales team?

Next you have to make sure you have put in place notifications or triggers that force you, as Sales Leader, to review and take some type of action. My recommendation is that changing an opportunity from non-qualified to qualified status is a great place to start. It shows the sales team they can freely enter new opportunities as they find them but until the key questions you want answered about things like dollar value, decision maker, timeline, etcetera have been completed it is not qualified and should not be quoted or a bunch of corporate resources committed to working on it expended. In my world, a non-qualified opportunity has a probability of winning of zero, so what this does is take a lot of pressure off the sales team to 'get the order'. They do have to advance the opportunity but this is often just between you and them and gives you great potential to have opportunity specific tactics discussions that are really superb coaching and mentoring sessions.

This is the mechanical, almost clerical part of forecasting. There is also the philosophical debate you must expect to constantly have with your team about when something goes into the CRM and starts getting 'tracked' with senior level visibility. On one hand, you will probably have members of your team that put everything into the CRM as part of an effort to show you they are constantly working to seek out new business. Under these circumstances, you need to be very methodical about reviewing their ratios; what percentage of what they enter ever closes in terms of both total dollar value and number of opportunities and things like that to make sure you are not blinded by a huge pipeline that has no basis in reality. On the other hand, there are lots of sales people who simply do not want to put anything in the CRM simply because they do not want the visibility, the questions and what they often perceive as micromanagement. I had one very successful salesperson actually tell me he would not put an opportunity into the CRM until he was highly confident it would close within a few weeks. In doing so, he provided no visibility to other things he was even working on. It is up to you to define what is or is not acceptable and use your authority to ensure it is being done.

The other issue you must take control of is to determine how the pipeline overall relates to actual revenue. There are some rules of thumb that some sales people like to go by but you have to be more methodical and precise about this and apply better weightings to be able to accurate turn a pipeline or forecast into an order. The most common is the three in one rule that basically says for every dollar in target you must have three dollars in qualified opportunities. Other similar rules of thumb include for every three meetings you have you will find one opportunity or for every three leads you get you can secure one meeting. Another school of thought is to apply a probability factor to each opportunity and only count that percentage of revenue. For example you have a $100,000 opportunity with a 50% probability of win so you apply $50,000. The problem with all these is they are too general or simplified. What I recommend is to track this very specifically over time and establish Key Performance Indicators that you can use to better manage your team. Some examples which I will expand on more at the end of Section 2 include number of sales calls per day or per week, number or dollar value of new opportunities created, number or dollar value of quotes issues against opportunities, time between finding opportunity and quoting, time between quoting and closing, etcetera. You can even track this for vertical markets, different key product or solution offerings and customer buying approaches like whether RFP based, three quote based or sole sourced.

When you have implemented all of this, and some of it will require superb management skills and the rest outstanding leadership abilities, you will be able to stand before your company and present a very real and compelling picture of what the future revenue looks like. Using KPIs will provide objective and not just a subjective view of the state of the world according to sales and give you the facts you need to justify everything from letting some go to adding a new position or getting more budget for travel.

Challenge #9 – Targets!

So much of how this affects you as Sales Leader is based on how targets are determined. In larger companies they are most often set by Executive Leadership and flow down with little to no opportunity for negotiation. In smaller organizations it is often more interactive with the outside sales team. Depending on your role, you may have an active part in defining the targets but you will have a critical role in delivering on all or some of them. It should be accepted that targets will increase year over year and unless you add more sales people or realign the territories, then that annual increase will also flow down. Most of the time, the increased target expectation is based on the greater of the previous target or the actual results.

Even if you do not have a direct role in determining the new targets, you do have a responsibility to present your recommendations to your Boss to ensure the views and perspectives of your Sales team are considered. If you have had a great year but a significant portion of that success was based on a program spend by one or two key customers that will not be repeating that spend in the next year, you need to make sure that is well understood. Perhaps the competitive landscape has changed, perhaps one or more of your key products have moved into the commodity side where both revenue and margin expectations need to be lowered, perhaps a key group of your customer base is government and there are expenditure freezes; all of these can have a dramatic impact on what the next year looks like.

In a perfect world you should be able to use your forecast to drive your target planning, but the reality is the forecast often provides a good look at the next one or two quarters with very limited visibility on the back half of the year. The longer your typical sales cycle, the greater your visibility further out will usually be but even this has limitations. My experience is that as much as Sales Leaders want to use a structure based approach to setting targets based on individual customer historical and anticipated buying patterns, the hard cold reality is CEOs tend to simplify things by saying something like "we will grow the business by x% next year." Your task is to figure out how to not just do that from a macro sense, but how to do it from a vertical market, territory and customer basis.

Let's be completely honest and accept that the behaviors of most sales people are driven by their compensation and mainly the variable commission or bonus income potential. Especially when there is an escalating variable plan driven by revenue or margin performance against target, the sales team will do everything they can to keep the targets low so they can over exceed and earn higher cheques. For a salesperson to be really successful they need to take ownership of their territory and their target. For that to happen, they not only have to buy into the target, they have to believe they can meet or exceed it and be willing to put in place a plan to do just that. If you impose a target they see as unrealistic or unachievable, they may outwardly go through the motions but do not be surprised if they give up. You could try to spin this by suggesting this is the best way forward but if you really believed that you would have initiated action to replace them already, so no matter how you slice it or dice it, you are faced with a vacant territory. That territory still has to meet a target and no matter how quickly you find a replacement there is a training period, extra demands on your time and all the other challenges associated with this situation.

I cannot really think of a time or situation where the Sales team were happy with the targets; it is one of those facts of life that you have to get very good at managing. Effectively you need to make the sale to your own team about not just why this is a fair and appropriate target (the steak) but that when they meet or exceed it look at how big their cheques will be (the sizzle). Rather than getting bogged down in justifying or rationalizing how the target was set, roll up your sleeves and get to work to put together a business plan with defined actions and executables that create a high probability for success. With the plan in place, add KPIs against which you will manage their progress. If you only base your assessment of their performance against how well they meet or exceed targets, you will probably find out too late that you have a problem they and possibly even you cannot recover from in time.

Challenge #10 – Sales Team Are Too Busy To Actually Sell

This happens a lot more than most realize, especially when you have a geographically dispersed Sales team. Most companies want their Sales team to spend the majority of their time in direct customer facing or interacting activities. To facilitate this, you have processes in place that define handoff points for things like quote preparation by Inside Sales or project workups by Product Management or Sales Engineering. Then you find out that all this is being done by an outside salesperson and when you ask them about it the answer is typically either "because I can do it faster myself" or "I could not get anyone to do it for me." As innocuous as this sounds, it can be one of the most difficult challenges for a Sales Leader. It crosses over multiple departments you may have no control over and creates many opportunities for your leadership to either shine or fade. Good sales people by nature tend to be control freaks. The more they exhibit this tendency, the more likely they are going to be reluctant to handoff to others, especially if the opportunity is significant or it is for a really key customer. And then, even if they do a handoff they usually do not really let it go and spend a lot of time and energy trying to figure out where it is and how they can keep it moving ahead. The ultimate result is that instead of doing customer facing activities they are doing company facing activities.

The other time this tends to happen is when your salesperson is highly knowledgeable about your products or solutions, not just from a features and benefits perspective, but from a technical and implementation point of view as well. Some companies want their sales people to be highly technical to the point of having Science or Engineering degrees but even in those cases there is still another higher level of technical expertise to back up Sales; sort of the generalist versus specialist situation.

So here is how it plays out. The salesperson has a great meeting with a customer and identifies a good opportunity. The salesperson may or may not take good notes but has enough to start the process to get a quote or proposal to the customer in a timely fashion. The customer has also asked for a description of the overall solution and perhaps even a drawing to show how this will fit into or work in their 'environment'. Rather than go to all the perceived 'hassle' of creating an opportunity in the CRM (which then might get noticed!), entering all the information and customer functional and technical requirements and then handing it off as per your defined processes, the salesperson just starts putting together the solution and preparing a proposal or quote. You only learn about this whole thing two or three days later when the salesperson vents to you that he cannot get any help from others to finish this off. Perhaps even worse is when the Engineering Manager comes to you asking why a design is being released to a customer that his team has not been involved with. In the meantime, the salesperson has spent most of the last couple days working on this and not really making other sales calls. He or she is probably taking incoming calls and dealing with emails and the like but this is a totally reactive and not proactive behavior that needs to be addressed.

So what do you do? You really only have two choices; either ignore this behavior, which effectively not only condones but confirms to Sales it is acceptable, or you take some type of corrective action which is once again a leadership opportunity for you. What you should not do is condone it or correct it based on who is doing it; that fundamentally means you are allowing a 'double standard' to exist which is a huge failure of leadership. Now I do not believe in the 'one size fits all' approach to anything so how you deal with this needs to be tempered to the individual. A relatively new salesperson might not really understand the processes well or gone through this so that is a fairly simply discussion, whereas a veteran might be a more serious and engaging conversation.

Just working on this issue with the salesperson does not necessarily solve the problem. A good part of the issue often stems from a lack of support from other departments or individuals you do not have any direct authority over. Now your 'play well in the sandbox' skills come into play as you work with your peers in these other departments to resolve core issues like supporting Sales, managing priorities related to customer expectations and delivering cost effective and technically compliant solutions in a timely manner. If you have not already figured this one out, it can be a very frustrating part of your day to day routine. It is made much easier when you are able to pre-position to your peer group what is coming at them in the next week or two so they can be better prepared to ensure their resources are available.

Notice it really has come back full circle to the salesperson in direct contact with the customer? If the salesperson provides early visibility of a pending customer requirement, documents the requirements and facilitates an effective handoff to the company, then you are in a much stronger position to keep everyone in the loop. This will ensure the customer gets what they need and when they need it, which is a critical part of all revenue generation. The message here is make sure you fix the issues in your department but also hold your peers accountable for their personnel as well.

Challenge #11 – Group Or Individual Meetings And How Often?

This is a loaded challenge because it follows the old saying 'you can please some of the people some of the time but you cannot please all of the people any of the time'[2]. Your Boss and your peers will have their preferred approach and your Sales team another. Actually, your Sales team would probably prefer they never have to participate in sales meetings, especially if they are group based and more than once a week. This is one situation where it is all or nothing, meaning you either do group meetings where everyone is expected to attend and participate, or you do individual meetings. No meetings is not really a viable option.

Daily group meetings first thing in the morning work for a lot of organizations that are retail or wholesale based and offer daily specials or attention grabbers. For outside professional sales teams, they can be effective if they are kept quite short and are more of a 'pump up' session and a way to make sure everyone is in on time and ready to go. Where they are more difficult to orchestrate is when the team is in multiple locations and multiple time zones. A very real issue is how much time they consume and efforts to keep them short will result in just skimming over the big stuff and ignoring the details. You can use it for a teaching lesson of the day but you have to recognize this is a shotgun approach that does not allow you to drill down on specific issues with specific people or to strategically or tactically brainstorm key opportunities or accounts.

Weekly group meetings allow you to allocate more time even if it is a couple hours and have it scheduled and locked into calendars well in advance. This extra time gives you the flexibility to work through all the key opportunities in each territory, brainstorm or confirm next steps and in one session have a complete view of the sales activity and plan. If you set it up like a mastermind or synergy group, there is less direct pressure on any individual and the potential for collaboration and better learning is very real. The tricky part is getting some of the team to really open up about what is happening in their territory, especially when progress since the last meeting has been limited, regardless of the reasons. When or if some of your team are remote it does make it more complicated, particularly when the meeting is long; you must expect some of the remote people will effectively tune out. If they are on a phone only voice link, it is pretty simple to mute their phone and do email or other tasks, all the while pretending to be active on the call. Going off mute and chiming in once in a while gives the appearance of participation when in truth they may not really be present. If you have the ability to use video conferencing of some type, it does keep most people more honest and engaged. If your team is large and spread internationally, you may be forced to do a couple of group meetings to try to keep the relative times of the meetings sort of within normal working hours.

Individual meetings allow you to really dig deep into what is going on in a territory but the issue is how much time it can eat up. In one position I held, we did Leadership and Executive meetings mid-week and to be fully prepared for these I spent a full day every week doing detailed individual meetings. By no means was this wasted time but it was time that was scheduled and required a lot of discipline to stay on course. If this is really the only time each week or period that you talk to each salesperson about what is going on, then you have to maximize what comes out of each call or meeting. If, on the other hand, you tend to talk to them every day or so as part of the normal process of getting things done, you probably already have a pretty good picture of what is going on in the territory and the formal weekly meeting is more of a confirmation.

Figuring out what will work for you is really only the first challenge; following through and making it work for your team and getting the information you need to report up is the really tough part.

Challenge #12 – Selling Versus Business Development

This is a much debated topic. For some people it is the same thing and they use the words interchangeably. Some even have Business Development titles to avoid any stigma of being in Sales. In larger organizations, they often have two independent groups sometimes headed by two different executives. For most, Sales is about direct customer interaction to deliver purchase orders to the company. Business Development is more about finding and creating new customers or taking new offerings to existing customers as an extension or add on to marketing activities. Another school of thought is that Sales is about direct to customer interactions whereas Business Development is about working through and with Partners who handle the direct customer touches.

Regardless of the definitions, every organization needs both to be done well if the business is to both thrive and grow. The real challenge is sorting out who does what, what the handoffs are and how people are compensated. Where this is particularly difficult is when you are a relatively small team and you have to do it all and so your folks wear a couple of hats. Remember the earlier discussion about compensation, as this is really where the rubber meets the road. If your variable compensation rewards monthly or quarterly results against targets, you must be prepared for a lack of real business development. This is even more pronounced when your sales cycles are already lengthy and the process to create new customers and gain initial sales success is many variable compensation cycles out in time. Most sales people will naturally default to working on more near term opportunities that will pay them in the short term, regardless of what you tell them they should be focussed on. By the way, be prepared to hear from your superiors that even when the variable compensation does not specifically cater to business development success, that it is part and parcel of their basic job and salary so they should be doing it anyway.

One thing to watch for is when you are being told what you want to hear. For example, in the weekly meetings your guys will tell you about all the emails and phone calls they are making to open up new doors, so you carry on happily believing there is lots of business development activity. As the Sales Leader you have to look a little more closely at two things in particular; how many actual meetings are taking place with these business development prospects and how many opportunities are being created that are further out in time than your typical averages. If your only key performance indicator is actual sales to new customers, you are going to be finding out way too late that there has not been any or enough business development and may find yourself having one of those less than comfortable conversations with your Boss.

Overall the best way to address this challenge is to ensure that you create expectations with your Sales team about what percentage of their time and effort must be spent on sales and business development. Just as important is that you also create the necessary key performance indicators to measure and manage those expectations.

Challenge #13 – Selling Or Business Development Versus Account Management

This is the Hunter (Sales or Business Development) versus Farmer (Account Management) debate all over again. As complex as true Account Management can be, there are many who suggest it is only for lazy sales professionals with the argument that "really how tough can it be to take care of a couple or few key accounts anyway?"

Good Account Managers wear many hats and are much more than just order takers. In any given day they can make a sale to an end user, negotiate pricing with procurement, resolve delivery issues with logistics, fix invoicing or billing problems with accounts receivable and schmooze senior executives as part of the long term relationship. They must be versatile in all these disciplines as the primary interface between the customer and your company. Also, they must be adept at working with senior and junior people and make them all feel important in the moment.

Really Good Account Managers are well versed in Sales, Business Development and all the things noted above. They also do three other things. They recognize that high value key accounts constantly have to be introduced to new products and services. They know new customer employees need to be 'educated' on your value proposition. In large customer organizations, new divisions or regions need to be opened up to grow the ongoing business.

A Top Performing Account Manager will have mapped out the customer organization, highlighted the key players with whom they must have relationships and have a targeted and dynamic plan for continuing repeat and creating new business. They will, often without having to look up specifics, know everything about every order in recent history and have a rock solid forecast of what is coming. When you start to hear "they don't provide forecasts" that is a cop out. Perhaps the customer does not formally provide forecasts but by meeting with all the key stakeholders and buyers on a regular basis, they can usually stick together a fairly accurate indication of what business is looming.

In my experience, very few sales professionals can be equally effective at both hunting and farming. As a Sales Leader, if you have expectations that your people will do both, you should be prepared for less than stellar results on both types of activities. Always be prepared to challenge the status quo; it is very common for Key Account Managers to tell you they are milking the cow for everything it can produce when in reality they are on cruise control. One interesting thing I have learned is that Account Managers are more reluctant than their Sales or Business Development counterparts to take their Sales Leaders into the Account to meet key stakeholders and decision makers. They are highly protective of their Key Accounts and maintain a bit of a mystery over what is going on in an effort to ensure they are seen as essential or even critical to keeping the revenue stream going.

Challenge #14 – Who Owns The Customer?

In my world, Sales owns the customer. What that really means is that Sales owns the customer relationship and experience. In smaller accounts where the interaction is typically with only one or two people, it is very simple, but in larger and more complex customer organizations that have distinct groups responsible for engineering, decision making, procurement, logistics, etcetera, the salesperson needs to be more of a conductor than a one-man band.

Sales is responsible for finding and generating revenue but even in a perfect world cannot realistically be expected to be the subject matter expert in all things. It is up to Sales to facilitate and manage the other conversations and interactions that occur between the customer team and your team. Sounds great in theory but in practise there are lots of chances for things to go horribly wrong.

In almost every case the problems happen when things are not well documented. If many different people are talking to one or more individuals representing the customer, there is potential for a lot of confusion over what has or has not been discussed or agreed to or even proposed. The CRM is the best place to track all the activity, emails, phone calls and the like but unless everyone is committed to using the CRM in a timely manner it will most likely be useless as an information or data repository and reference. What it boils down to is that if you do not have an efficient and effective way to communicate internally about a customer and their opportunity, you are going to experience challenges, not just in winning the business but also in delivering on your commitments.

Beyond really good internal communications you must have a good way to 'handoff' responsibilities between departments based on what is happening with the customer. Sometimes Sales needs the Engineering team to get directly involved with the customer to finalize the solution to be proposed or provided. Sometimes Operations needs to contribute in terms of manufacturing or delivery lead times. Sometimes Accounting needs to approve new credit terms. All of this can happen as part of the sales process well before an actual order is received. Sales is typically highly motivated to get all this in place or completed but what happens when the order is received?

Sales cannot walk away saying "we did our job" just because the order was received, but rather needs to maintain vigilance over the process until the project is complete, the invoicing has been done and the payment has been received. Having said this, an order is a great way to handoff from Sales to Operations. This assumes Sales has provided all the necessary backup information like quotes or proposals and their underlying workups to the Ops team, who now have to move ahead with entering the order and initiating any purchasing or manufacturing that needs to be done to fulfill the order. What about the Engineering or Service teams that may have a role to play in the order fulfillment; who gets them involved, when and what supporting information needs to be provided to them so they can do their jobs? All of these are critical internal processes that must be in place, but once again I believe that if Sales does not keep an eye on what is happening, it is not uncommon for something to fall through the cracks.

It really does all come down to having the internal processes and communications in place that will allow Sales to own the relationship without getting so bogged down that they cannot do other sales activities. This is truly the challenge and responsibility of the Sales Leader to handle.

Challenge #15 – Chasing Money!

Just because Sales owns the customer does not mean it is a good thing when the salesperson trying to get the next order has to chase unpaid invoices. This does not typically happen in public or larger private companies but in small and medium sized companies, especially when the owner is active in the business, this is not at all infrequent. What usually happens is Accounts Receivable will do a report showing accounts past due 30 or 60 days and express frustration at either not getting good answers from the account or getting answers or commitments that are not fulfilled.

This plays out in a couple of different ways. The first is when either the owner or CFO comes to you or goes directly to the salesperson responsible for the account and asks if you or they can assist in getting it taken care of. My advice is that the Sales Leader and salesperson have a quick chat to figure out how to best take care of this. If the Sales Leader has good personal contacts in the Account, it is probably better he or she make the call and completely isolate the salesperson from the situation. If the salesperson has contacts with the administration, accounting or logistics teams within the Account, this is a good approach remembering what you really want to avoid is talking to those who either recommend or commit to buying from you.

The second and much more business dangerous thing that can happen is someone makes a decision to hold pending orders until the account is back in good standing, without informing sales. I have seen this occur, even when the account in question is a key account that is normally not in arrears. Without warning, someone follows the rule and not the intent of the rule and creates a mess. Good business practises dictate that accounts in arrears need to be effectively managed, including insisting on full or partial prepayments or holding existing shipments and the like, but these should be considered last ditch measures not invoked without discussion and understanding the implications.

Challenge #16 – Who Owns Price And Margin?

Unless you are in a very high volume, low margin distribution type business, if the only conversation you are having is about prices then you are probably having the wrong conversation, maybe with the wrong person. So we are on the same page, I define cost as the amount you have into or pay for a product or service. Price is the amount the customer pays you for that product or service. Value is the intangible amount included in the price (not the cost) of the product or service that should allow you to command a higher price than your competitor.

In most companies, both margin and revenue are important but margin is usually most important as it determines how much you have to actually run the business and turn a profit. Target margins are usually decided at the Executive Management level with very strict guidelines or even rules on what must happen to bid or quote below those target margins. If a salesperson can command a higher price and higher margin without creating a concern that you are overpriced or worse gouging, then that usually does not require much oversight. Given the critical nature of achieving minimum target margins which are controlled and managed from the top down and given that the price charged to a customer is really just a calculated value based on margin, margin and price are really owned by the Company.

Having said this, Sales has a very important role in determining what the price should be. That role is to bring to the decision discussion as much relevant customer based information as possible. Other disciplines like Marketing and Product Management should have done extensive market analysis to provide competitive offerings and their actual and relative costs, but in the absence of the customer perspective, the pricing conversation can be purely theoretical or academic.

As Sales Leader, it is your responsibility to ensure your sales people are having this type of discussion with your customers. For most, this can be a very difficult conversation to have; it is like discussing your salary or commission plan with your Boss where nobody is usually really comfortable and happy until the conversation is over. When you ask your sales people about whether they have had the pricing chat with their customers, do not be surprised if the answer is typically something like "they are not prepared to discuss pricing." Here is a tip; that is often code for "I did not have the conversation about pricing." The way to overcome the challenges of this conversation is to make it just part of the ongoing dialogue by asking simple questions like:

1. Are you already buying this now? And depending on the answer here are some standard follow on questions,
    a. Is it doing everything you need it to do?
    b. Are you happy with the price you are paying?
    c. What price would you like to pay?
    d. If I could supply an alternative would you be open to a demo or trial or quote (fill in the right one depending on the circumstance)?
2. If you are not buying something now to solve this problem, why not or what would it take to get you to buy what I have?
3. Always the fun question – what is more important, price or value? If you are going to ask this, you better be real good at articulating your full value proposition.

The bottom line is that Sales does not usually own price or margin but the defendable customer intelligence you bring to the discussion can impact both quite dramatically. Just saying you need to be cheaper to win the business without some meat on that bone just shows how little you really know about the actual situation and how poor your relationship is with the customer, not something I would want to be demonstrating too often.

Challenge #17 – I Need It Today!

If I just had a dime for every time I heard that one! Sometimes something is urgent and must go to the front of the line but most of the time this is simply not the case. What the salesperson will do is create the impression that if you do not get it done today, the customer will be upset with you or buy from someone else or quit buying from us. That will simply supercharge the level of import and stress into a situation that requires neither if effectively handled.

On the surface this does not seem to be much of an issue but what you have to realize is the knock-on effect this kind of issue can create. Sales people harassing other departments to get them to drop everything they are working on to respond to a priority does not usually generate goodwill. The other question to ask is, if I stop everything else to respond to this request, what is not getting done that might be a higher value or higher priority or both? Outside Sales people typically have tunnel vision and can only see and understand what is happening in their territory; they often have little to no perspective on what the overarching priorities really are.

This demand for priority usually is for a quote or to get a shipment out the door. In the case of a quote I usually ask "are they issuing the order today?" and that usually stops this thing dead. In the case of it must ship today I ask "what happens if it does not ship until tomorrow?" Most of the time this need for urgency is because someone screwed up and they now need a favour to get something back on track. If this is a once in a while occurrence from this salesperson or that customer, you can easily accommodate it in this situation. As a Sales Leader, what you have to watch for are patterns or bad habits that could be developing, especially if it is an internal problem.

Challenge #18 – What Is A Good Sales Call?

One of the Key Performance Indicators often tracked for Sales people is how many 'good' sales calls did they complete in a day or a week or other time period. There are many who believe there is a direct and unequivocal correlation between the number of good sales calls completed and success in a territory, where success is simply defined as meeting or exceeding revenue and margin targets. At one extreme, a good sales call is one that is scheduled in advance, planned in detail and executed flawlessly in a face to face meeting with the customer. At the other extreme, I have had sales people tell me a well-crafted email should count.

Before weighing in on the pros and cons of what makes a good sales call, you first have to make sure that what your Sales team is doing and is being measured against, is aligned with your company 'Go to Market Strategy'. Your Go to Market Strategy (GTMS) is a high level strategy that comes right from the top on how you will be staffed and resourced to penetrate the market to win business. Your GTMS defines how leads are identified and who is responsible for this, how leads are contacted and how the sales process flows. Taken to the next level, the GTMS also shows the correlation and relationships between the various intercompany departments, where the handoffs occur and who is responsible to who and for what.

As an example, I worked with one company where the President was unwavering in his expectation that every outside salesperson would do 4-6 planned and meaningful sales calls every day and it was his belief that these were almost all face to face meetings. A friend of mine sells cleaning supplies and has a significant customer base over a large geographic area; his daily routine is to pick a local area within the region and go out and drop in and visit with his customers about once every month or so. He has no problem completing 4-6 sales calls a day and in the process shows new products, leave samples to try, takes orders and solves any issues the customer is having. Based on leads he gets from his company, he even finds time to organize scheduled calls with potential new customers while in a local area. Fairly routine and fairly simple and my friend loves his job, the flexibility he has to control his own schedule and effectively control his income as he is 100% commission based. Contrast this with a salesperson who sells complex technical solutions to customers who restrict access without scheduled appointments and is responsible for a territory that covers many States or Provinces and it is a completely different situation.

It is my opinion that a good sales call is one that gets you closer to a sale. It might be a phone call, a face to face or a webinar. I do not consider emails a sales call but rather use them as part of the continuing touch process with customers to keep the conversation alive, provide information and schedule the actual sales calls. One of the challenges I have faced is I call someone to try to make an appointment and they say something like "I have a few minutes now so let's just talk now instead of making an appointment", so I tend to try to use email to set appointments and avoid the brush off, especially if I really want the meeting to be in person.

As the Sales Leader one of your primary responsibilities is to make sure your sales team are meeting their sales call expectations based on your GTMS. When revenue is up and margins are good you have a bit of room to manoeuvre but when the opposite is true you will be held to account. The best advice is to preach and practise it every day, track it rigourously and when necessary take whatever preventative, corrective or congratulatory action is needed.

Challenge #19 – Joint Sales Calls For Mentoring And Coaching

I am a very strong believer in using joint sales calls to meet key customers and either train or evaluate the performance of your sales people. Nothing can replace direct interaction with a customer to tell you what they are really thinking and how they do business. You also get to see your salesperson in action from setting up to planning and conducting a meeting.

Joint sales calls are a great tool to train new sales people. Rather than simply telling them what is expected, go with them and show them. Assuming you know the account and the customer, this is a simple way to handoff this account to the new salesperson and help set them up for success. It gives you the chance to get direct updates on all the existing opportunities with this customer and to find out what else is possible over the next while.

I particularly like to use joint sales calls to go out and work with a member of my team who is struggling a bit before it becomes too serious, especially if this person is remote from you. It forces them to fill their calendar for a few days and that by itself creates a renewed focus on what is going on in their Territory. The number one objective I always set for these appointments is to find new opportunities. To that end, I insist that these appointments target key accounts that typically have a good flow of business or potential new customers and I also want to meet the decision makers wherever possible.

As valuable as the meeting with the customer is, the after meeting discussion you and your salesperson have about the meeting is where some of the best value comes out. They get to ask you questions about how or why you went down a specific path, you get to brainstorm about what is next with this customer and you get to offer specific feedback, advice or otherwise to your salesperson about their 'performance' during the meeting.

It is not uncommon for sales types to push back when you ask them to set up meetings for you to join, especially when the meetings are with the more or most senior people they engage with in the customer organization.

This push back is more pronounced if they have been unable to get you answers to things about what is going on in the account. Typically, they are worried about either being exposed for not having asked the right questions or the answers they have provided are very different from what you find out when you ask the questions. You have to be careful to not do an 'end run' on your own salesperson and set the appointment yourself but if your salesperson continues to object to the meeting or is unable to set the meeting this might be exactly what you have to do, only after advising your salesperson that is what you are doing. This usually finds them getting the meeting in a very short period of time, albeit quite begrudgingly.

Try a few of these joint calls and I am absolutely convinced you will discover how powerful they can be for both the customer and your salesperson. By ultimately giving the salesperson credit for everything that comes from the meetings, you reinforce for them that your interests are helping them be successful to the benefit of the Company.

Challenge #20 – Managing The Training Gap

Ongoing training is critical to the success of any sales team and it is up to the Sales Leader to set the pace for training. Too many companies only conduct training for new product or service introductions, ignoring the need for regular sales training, in an effort to continually improve overall sales team performance. Like many other issues, if your sales team is geographically dispersed this is more of a challenge, but with all the collaboration tools available today this is simply a complication and not a real show stopper.

First and foremost, you have to identify what gap or gaps exist in the training of your sales team. There is no 'one size fits all' approach to sorting out who needs what training, rather as the Sales Leader it is up to you to be continually monitoring each of them on a very personal basis to determine what training is required. There is an old adage that 'success leaves clues' and the converse of this is equally true, namely that a lack of success also leaves clues as to where a salesperson is struggling.

This is where having and using a series of Key Performance Indicators (KPIs) can really be helpful. Tracking things like number of sales calls, number and value of new opportunities and strength of pipeline will all give you indicators of where someone is strong or weak. Getting even more granular and looking at these on a service or product type basis can highlight a salespersons issues with a specific product or offering that could simply be addressed with training. Use the KPIs to help plan the joint sales call frequency you do with your sales team, whether they are local or remote.

Once you have identified what training needs to be conducted it is much simpler and more efficient to put in place a program to address the training gap. You can do it on a team basis with structured and scheduled sessions or you can do it on an individual basis; whatever works best for your specific situation. The real message here is that unless every salesperson on your team is hitting and exceeding their targets, there is no excuse for not putting in place a training system of some sort.

Challenge #21 – Having An Effective And Efficient CRM

You must have a Customer Relationship Manager. The majority of companies already have a CRM of some type and you have to adapt and work with it, often with limited ability to make substantial changes. I was fortunate in a recent position that the company had purchased a CRM but it had not been implemented, so I had the chance to champion what and how was ultimately deployed.

A real CRM is much more than a contact management system or digital Rolodex; it must be a fully integrated platform that pulls together contacts, accounts and opportunities and connects to email, calendars and other corporate enterprise software solutions. The really good CRMs also include or can integrate with phone systems, quoting software and can be accessed while on a smartphone or tablet while mobile.

Although every department in the company should have access to and use the CRM, the core of it is really about managing your customer interactions. To ever expect sales people to enthusiastically embrace a CRM is probably wishful thinking, however if the CRM is implemented from a Sales perspective and offers benefits to the Sales team, they will use it.

Your number one CRM challenge is that the CRM offers little direct benefit to the individual sales people who perceive it as a management tool. At its worst, the CRM is seen by sales people as a 'big brother' tool that management uses. To overcome these, either perceived or real limitations, you have to do what you can to focus on what the direct benefits to using the CRM will be to the Sales team and work with management to upgrade or customize what the CRM offers to Sales. Things that matter to the Sales team typically include calendar and task reminders, ease of access and use from both in and out of the office and opportunity management. What the Sales team most of all does not like is when every customer interaction has to be logged, not to provide comprehensive notes on the status of specific accounts, customers or opportunities but because it is a way for management to measure how busy the salesperson is or has been.

Challenge #22 – Which Came First – Your Sales Process Or Your CRM?

This one is going to be short and quite blunt. As a follow on to the challenge of having a CRM is the issue of which came first. If the sales process you follow is based on what the CRM is capable of supporting and not actually reflective of the process your team follows, then you have a problem of massive proportions. When I first started to implement our CRM where I was Sales Leader and overall responsible for the project, it was quite amazing the pressure I was under from the software integration company we contracted to 'adjust' my sales process to fit the CRM environment rather than the other way around.

If your sales process does not work then fix it. If your sales process is being driven by the limitations of the CRM, then either make changes to the CRM or change the CRM entirely. If, as Sales Leader, you cannot make the internal sale to get the funding necessary to make the CRM improvements needed, then you have to have a heart to heart conversation with yourself about how truly committed you are to either the sales process or CRM or both!

Challenge #23 – How Do You Manage Really Long Sales Cycles?

I consider anything longer than three months a long sales cycle, although I have plenty of experience with cycles much longer than that. Regardless, really long sales cycles are typically associated with very high value projects. It is not uncommon for many government related procurements to take a very long time as the budgeting and approval processes can be very involved and multi-faceted, even if the total value of the project or procurement is not really that large. If a budget manager failed to include a capital acquisition in the current year budget and the requirement is not an 'emergency', the purchase can easily be delayed until the following budget year.

On the surface many people would simply suggest that you just put the opportunity in the CRM, stay as close to it as possible over the necessary timeframe and eventually you will get the business. However, you have to contrast this one dimensional view of the business with the reality that you have a Sales team that is probably incented on a monthly or quarterly basis so they are going to focus on what is going to pay them now and not six, twelve or eighteen months from now. An easy way to check this is to have a good hard look at your own CRM and ask how reliable and confident are you of your pipeline beyond the next incentive periods?

The issue is not how much do you believe in what is in the pipeline beyond a certain date, but is the pipeline really reflective of the amount of business available to you beyond that date? When your Sales team is focused on the next quarter because that is how they are incented, they tend to not even take the time and effort to identify new opportunities that are more than a couple quarters out. Even when they do find them, they tend to not spend as much time working on them early because they are a lower priority than chasing the opportunity they can close next week.

Your Sales team must know how every customer manages their budgets and whether what they buy from you is out of capital or operations and maintenance funds. Beyond this your team must work to find out from their personal contacts in the customer organization what purchases or projects are planned in the current year that you might be able to sell or at least compete for. The further out the project, the less clear even the customer will probably be on many of the specifics but at least you have early visibility of what might be coming and when. This is the art of building a pipeline and all of this can be tracked and managed using the CRM.

As the Sales Leader, the easiest way to get this type of longer term visibility on projects is to encourage your team that when they are working with customers on immediate and short term orders, to ask the customer what might be developing that is longer term. Sometimes it can be simple a question as "any projects starting up that might be a while in developing that I might be able to assist you with?" Customers may tell you what they know or the person you are dealing with may simply say they do not know but you can talk to Mary or Bob about that and you now have a referred lead.

The other thing you have to do as Sales Leader is to continually monitor the pipeline and ensure your team is finding and reporting on longer term opportunities. Many sales people will try to avoid putting in longer term opportunities because they do not want to create too much visibility on things further out, when in reality they should be coached into getting it on the pipeline so it takes the pressure off them.

Long sales cycle business requires more patience and flexibility by sales, sales management and executive management. At some point longer term opportunities do become short term opportunities where there is a lot more clarity on exactly what is required, what the actual budget is and when the order will be placed. In the interim, it is quite common for dates to shift, priorities to change and budgets to be adjusted due to many different factors. As Sales Leader, the best way to overcome this is to simply have as many of them on the books as possible and keep them current by having specific tactics in place for each, all the while ensuring executive management does not count on them as slam dunks.

Challenge #24 – Selling Vapourware – Cannibalizing Your Sales

New products or services can create a lot of excitement for any company but only if introduced properly. Sales people are always looking for new stuff to take to their customers, however there must be a balance between what can be delivered today and what you have to wait for. As Sales Leader, it is your responsibility to stand firmly between the company and your Sales team and ensure your Sales team stays totally focused on selling real products and services and not be 'wasting' time and energy on so-called vapourware.

There are really two types of new products and services; those that are completely new and different from anything your company currently offers and those that are 'new and improved' versions of existing offerings with added features and benefits. Although neither should be introduced to the market until ready for 'primetime', it is the upgraded products that can create the greatest risk for cannibalization, where a customer who may have purchased today decides to wait for the upgraded version before buying. What is even worse is when the new product misses the intended launch date and revenue is pushed back weeks or months. You can go back to the customer to try to get them to buy the available product now but unless you give them an awesome deal you probably will not be able to change their mind. You also risk them looking for a competing product that offers what the now late new product was supposed to provide.

At some point all new products should go through some type of market testing to gauge interest and get feedback but this should be a highly managed process between Marketing, Product Management and Sales. Customers are carefully selected based on the relationship, their input into the new product and their complete understanding of the process and how it will unfold. In the absence of such an orchestrated plan the Sales Leader must push back on the company to ensure sales cycles and real sales are not lost or significantly delayed.

Challenge #25 – How Do You Manage Competitive Differentiation?

If you do not have competition you are either wildly successful already or in the wrong business! Competition is a fact of life but losing to it or losing sleep over it is up to you. To be successful against competition, your Sales team must be able to clearly and concisely articulate what differentiates your offering from the competition, especially if there is a significant price difference.

If price is the only thing that matters to the customer and you do not have the lowest price you simply have to accept that and move on. If the customer is really interested in a price and value discussion then you must be prepared and capable of carrying that conversation. Most often this will require you to be able to contrast and compare the competition's offering as well.

You can only go so far with the old sales technique of saying "I really do not know a lot about the competition and although I am sure they have a good product, let me tell you why mine is the best." At some point and especially when the customer is either technical or looking for ways to justify buying something more expensive or more feature rich, you will invariably be asked "how does your solution or product compare to the other guys?" You can only defer or deflect those soft objections for so long before your customer will lose patience and move on.

It is typically the responsibility of Marketing and/or Product Management to prepare and keep updated competitor analyses, whether they be written documents or simple matrix tables. As Sales Leader, it is your responsibility to work with these other groups to get this done but unless you have nobody doing Marketing or Product Management it is not your work to do independently.

Section 2 Bonus – Sales Key Performance Indicators

There are very many different KPIs you can use to track the performance of your team, which are typically referred to as either leading or lagging. To identify whether an indicator is leading or lagging, you first have to define what you are trying to 'indicate'. For Sales I would suggest that it is all about revenue so leading indicators are those which provide visibility on things or activities that lead to revenue and lagging are those which are based on post purchase order activities or things.

Leading Sales KPIs

1. Number of scheduled appointments. This can be tracked in either a calendar or CRM. It provides visibility on upcoming meetings and can be further refined to show either first time appointments with new prospects or potential customers or follow up meetings with existing accounts.
2. Number of completed appointments. Best tracked in the CRM by reviewing after meeting notes entered.
3. Number of new opportunities created. This will come from the CRM but with this you can also look at
   a. How many total completed appointments to create an opportunity, on average.
   b. How many total appointments within a specific account to create an opportunity.
4. Value of new opportunities created. This comes from the CRM and allows you to also track
   a. Average value of opportunities per meeting.
   b. Total value of opportunities.
5. Number and value of quotes created and issued. This comes from the CRM and allows you to also track
   a. Time between first meeting and quote.

      b.   Accuracy between estimate opportunity value and actual quote, recognizing that your longer term revenue forecast is usually based on the opportunity value well before a quote is finalized.

      c.   Total value of outstanding quotes.

6. Strength of pipeline. With all the information properly entered into your CRM you can now do a pipeline analysis. Many sales team have different 'offerings' and are required to meet targets against each offering or product grouping so you can develop a method or matrix that take the pipeline data from the CRM and look at it from multiple perspectives including

      a.   Total value of pipeline and average value per qualified or quoted opportunity.

      b.   Factored value of pipeline which, in its simplest form, multiplies the value of the opportunity by its probability of win. For example a $10,000 opportunity with a 50% probability contributes $5,000 to the factored pipeline.

      c.   Pipeline or factored pipeline versus total target or period (monthly or quarterly) target on a product, offering or total basis.

Lagging Sales KPIs

There is really only one real lagging KPI and that is the number and value of Purchase Orders. In Sales this is really what you are being measured against and with orders in hand you can now use the information gathered from the leading indicators to do any number of analytical comparisons and here are my favourites

1. Revenue versus margin including averages and even broken out by product or offering.
2. Revenue versus target including any number of time based windows like month or quarter.

3. Number and percentage of quotes won.
4. Number and value of actual revenue versus opportunities.
5. Average revenue per meeting.

The options are really endless but it really comes down to two things
1. How do you report this information?
2. How do you use this information to work with your team?

My recommendation is that you use different reports for your Boss or the Executive team than you use for your team. Your superiors tend to want to verify the activity level of your team and value of the closable opportunities will meet or exceed targets. Your ability to demonstrate this in the simplest terms will keep the pressure off of you to get into too much detail most of the time.

What I liked to do with my Sales team was to put together a fairly comprehensive report that showed
1. Actual Invoiced and Total Backlog against target by offering.
2. Total Pipeline against current shortfall to target (factoring in the revenue and backlog) for both current and next fiscal period.
3. Total Factored Pipeline against current shortfall to target for both current and next fiscal period.
4. Review these numbers against upcoming planned and scheduled activities and have specific tactical discussions on what it will take to close and deliver the revenue to meet or exceed the targets.

Section 3 - Sales Thoughts and Ideas

For many years I have written a Sales Thought of the Day based on a Theme of the Week. Many of these themes and thoughts were based on commonly used quotes and clichés but very many were original ideas. In all cases an effort was made to use the daily thought to offer perspective, context or advice relevant to my sales team.

Here is my personal favourite and one I woke up in the middle of the night to write down and gives you an example of what will follow

IF YOU ARE NOT PREPARED TO GIVE UP WHAT YOU'VE GOT
TO GET WHAT YOU REALLY WANT
YOU WILL HAVE TO JUST KEEP WHAT YOU'VE GOT
WHETHER YOU LIKE IT OR NOT!

The remainder of this book will be a comprehensive presentation of these themes and thoughts broken down into a number of sections including

1. Planning
2. Key Accounts
3. Team Player
4. Sales Basics
5. Process and Prospecting
6. Closing
7. Dealing with Adversity
8. Be a Great Example
9. Elevate and Motivate

I encourage you to use these in your daily sales leader lives. Feel free to adapt or adjust these thoughts and ideas into mentoring or teaching points for your sales teams.

Planning

MOST PEOPLE DO NOT PLAN TO FAIL,
THEY JUST FAIL TO PLAN[3]

I start with this one, which some attribute to Ben Franklin and others to John Beckley, because it really is tried and true. Let me give you a heads up about me on this topic. My wife and close friends will tell you I never stop planning; this is something the Army hammered into me and I do it continually and for everything. I can plan formally and in meticulous detail or I can plan on the fly. The truth; I am not a particularly spontaneous guy and planning is second nature to me and I do not see it as an onerous or frustrating task.

The sad reality is most people spend more time planning their annual vacation than their retirement. What that speaks to is the idea or philosophy that it is easy to commit time and effort to planning for fun but anything not fun related is suddenly a challenge.

From a Sales perspective, you and your team should have plans for everything. You should have a plan for how you are going to meet your target, you should have a plan for each major account, you should have a plan for each key opportunity, and you should have a plan for what you are going to do tomorrow and so on and so on. I cannot even guess how many joint sales calls I have gone out to with members of my sales team where they did not even have a plan for what they wanted to accomplish in the sales meeting.

Some plans need to be fairly comprehensive and written down and others are quite simple and less formal. An annual business plan is an example of the former and a sales call an example of the latter. In the absence of a plan, you are betting your success on luck or circumstance or a combination of both and that does not typically bode well for long term employment.

THE BEST PLANS NEVER SURVIVE FIRST CONTACT!

Planning is not a panacea and will not guarantee success. Very few plans unfold exactly as expected. Here is the key; by taking the time and making the effort to plan properly you look at the variables, you look at the factors that affect the plan and you look at the options open to you. Go back and review the example of the decision making process at the end of the first Section. By having completed this detailed analysis as part of the planning process, you are better positioned to manage the challenges when the plan goes off track.

If your plan is to drive from point A to point B and you find out halfway there that part of your route is blocked, it could be as simple as making a planned detour based on your prior route analysis and knowledge of traffic patterns. In the business of sales and sales leadership it is not quite as simple; you may have to shift your business development focus, you may have to reassign staff resources or add new staff, you may have to do more customer meetings, etcetera. Again, the key is that by working through a detailed plan and understanding where you expect your business to come from, and what it will take to deliver that revenue, you are better able to respond (and not just react) to the deviations you will encounter.

The next time one of your team members tells you they just lost a significant opportunity they were counting on just ask them "what are you going to do to replace that revenue?" If their answer is "I need to think about it" or "I guess I will have to find another customer to sell to" or anything less than "I was counting on that one to close but my pipeline is strong and I have lots of other opportunities I can focus on winning", then you know this sales person has no plan and is winging it.

THINK STRATEGICALLY, ACT TACTICALLY

Sometimes you get so wrapped up in the day to day that you forget what you are really trying to accomplish overall. It reminds me of the old adage 'you cannot see the forest for the trees'! When you develop your plan, you have to be completely in sync with the intent of your Company. When faced with a local challenge, whether it be account, customer, product, service or support based, you have to keep in mind what the higher level strategic plan is. You must ensure that when you solve your challenge it does not contradict or clash with what you are collectively working to achieve.

So let's bring it down one level. Your Company plan is to achieve defined revenue and gross margin targets and on a year over year basis grow by a defined percentage. Your Territory (strategic) plan will be to achieve defined revenue and gross margin targets on both a quarterly and annualized basis. Your variable compensation is most likely driven by your ability to meet or exceed those targets.

You develop your plan based on specific revenue targets in each account or customer and for each product offering. At the macro level, you need a strategic plan for each account but how you actually manifest that plan into actionable activities and work is your tactical plan. Think of the Strategic Plan as the *WHAT* and the Tactical Plan as the *HOW*.

As you start the process of building your overall plan you must take the time to do a detailed review of each account or customer. You must understand what they have purchased in the past and you must know what they might be able to purchase in the future. If you already know about a number of programs or projects or planned buys that is easy; just plug in those numbers against the right timeline and you are off to a great start. The real work is in figuring out where the rest of the revenue will come from and what you have to do to make that happen.

Oh, and in most businesses, it is not good enough to have just enough in the pipeline to meet the target. For all the undefined revenue you may need 5-10 times as much potential in the pipeline.

PLAN METICULOUSLY, EXECUTE FLAWLESSLY

A plan is not worth the paper it is printed on if it is not well executed! Far too many plans are written simply to be able to say there is a plan but then it gets put on the shelf and people wonder why targets were missed. Once you have an approved or agreed upon plan (*THE WHAT*), the next and most critical part of the process is to prepare to execute the plan (*THE HOW*). As a minimum, you need to break this down into specific action items and tasks for each account or customer and for each offering.

You should always have more executable items to take care of than there is time to complete them. This forces you to take a few minutes on an ongoing basis to prioritize your items based on what will get you closer to achieving your overarching Strategic intent. Far too often people will do the easiest items first even though those items really have little net effect on creating significant revenue. Throw in the added complications of unexpected customer calls or other customer related challenges and your day can be messed up before you seem to have accomplished anything. It is only by having a clearly defined plan that you can make the necessary 'on the fly' adjustments to stay on track for success.

As a Sales Leader, you have to watch for when your sales team appears to be constantly overwhelmed by the number of critical items on their action list. Take the time to complete a review with your sales person and assist them to manage their workload by resetting priorities or having things handed off to inside sales or other departments. On the flip side, you need to watch for when sales people seem really busy but are not accomplishing anything. It is too easy to slip into account management mode where they spend the majority of their time taking care of a few key accounts and waiting for the phone to ring or an email to arrive. When and if they have some downtime they should be able to pull out a task list for account or business development and immediately start to make calls and generate activities that will lead to new revenue. Without the plan and without the go-to list, the downtime becomes a burden and loss of sales cycles.

WHAT IS YOUR PERSONAL SUCCESS RATIO?

You need to know this as it has a direct impact on how you complete your business planning. For every ten face to face meetings you conduct with prospects or customers, how many of these generate opportunities? These opportunities may not be qualified and they may ultimately not lead to revenue, but as you come out of a meeting can you specifically identify one or more opportunities where the customer has a problem and is prepared to spend money and you have products or solutions to offer?

Based on this ratio, you should very easily be able to identify how many separate meetings with one or more people in a customer organization are needed to generate sufficient pipeline potential revenue to meet or exceed your target. If you have lots of time and experience with a list of accounts and customers within those accounts, you may be able to even refine your ratio based on the account or customer. For new account acquisition or business development efforts, you also need to figure out what your ratio is for turning leads or prospects into opportunities and eventually customers and often this ratio will be lower. For example, you may find for every three meetings you have with an existing account you identify one new opportunity but for new business it might take six or seven meetings to find an opportunity. This speaks directly to the importance of building a relationship and developing trust.

Do not plan on waiting for customers to phone or email you to tell you they have a problem and need to buy something, as in my direct sales career that strategy has not worked very well overall. Yes, you will always get some revenue from that but you cannot base your business plan on expecting the customer to contact you.

THE FUNDAMENTALS OF A WELL PREPARED BUSINESS PLAN

This is not really as complex a task as most people suspect but it does require some quiet think time to be able to do it well. Personally, I do not look for a long wordy document describing market conditions, local trends and the like; rather I want to see an account by account breakdown of what is going to be required to meet the target objectives.

For each account,

1. What is the target revenue? The sum of all your accounts should be your total target. Anything less means you have to either increase the expected revenue from some or all your accounts or you have to create new accounts.

2. To achieve this revenue in this account and based on a minimum 3 to 1 ratio, what is the total of all my opportunities in the pipeline for this account?

3. What specific actions need to be taken to move these opportunities along in the pipeline?

    a. Are they qualified?

    b. What is the probability of closure?

    c. Do I need to set up a demo or technical support sales call?

    d. Do I need technical support to prepare solution options for consideration and discussion?

    e. Do I need to prepare a proposal or quotation?

    f. Do I need to schedule a face to face follow up?

    g. Do I need to ask for the order?

4. If the opportunity total is less than the 3 to 1 ratio, what is the difference and based on this difference:

    a. Based on the average order I get from this account, how many new opportunities must I have to meet the difference?

    b. How many sales calls must I set up with one or more representatives in this account to find/identify/uncover these new opportunities?

c. Who do I need to meet with and by when to make this happen?

In the end, what you are really putting together is a structured list of planned sales calls that you need to make over the next 30-120 days to get your pipeline where it needs to be. This will give you the confidence that as you work your pipeline, you will deliver or exceed the expected revenue and associated margin.

You can and should do this exercise to begin a new year, at the beginning of each quarter and even as often as once a month. Compare your results to your plan and see where you have had success and where you could have done better. Self-critique and self-evaluate and make changes to your routine and habits and you will be astonished at the improvement in your overall results.

TAKE OWNERSHIP OF YOUR PLAN

Whether you are the Sales Leader or a Sales Account Manager, the final and perhaps the most important part of the business planning process is that you take complete responsibility and ownership of your plan. The plan is a combination of the targets and the specific strategy and tactics that have to be executed for you to be successful this year or quarter or month.

Targets are very often imposed from above, along with how variable compensation is paid. Even as Sales Leader, you often have input but very little control over either of these programs. Often your first reaction to the targets and possible income will be 'too high and too low' respectively. If you cannot get beyond that to not just accept these imposed numbers but speak to them as if you created them, then you are not being true and loyal to your company.

As a salesperson, you always dread the day new targets are released. You can hope that the assigned targets are based on historical performance and some measure of thoughtfulness and include input from the Sales department but that is not always the case. In the end you have to embrace these targets and take complete ownership of them by developing a business plan that will get you where you need to go in terms of both revenue and margin generation.

There will be a whole section later devoted to the importance of Attitude for Sales Professionals but suffice it to say here that if you try to build a plan believing you will not succeed then this old adage comes true once again, namely

If you think you can, you can
If you think you can't, you are right!

THE IMPORTANCE OF GOAL SETTING

As you are very aware, there are literally dozens and dozens of books on this subject so I will only offer a few thoughts on this.

Goals Must Be Realistic And Achievable But They Must Also Be Hard To Reach

When setting goals you must find a balance between what is unachievable and what is so simple there is no challenge. Andrew Carnegie said "If you want to be happy, set a goal that commands your thoughts, liberates your energy and inspires your hopes."[4]

Minimalist goals create minimalist actions and minimalist results and the converse is also true; top performers and overachievers innately understand this and set 'reach' goals in their personal and professional lives.

Goals Must Be Written Down And Revisited Regularly

As Mark Victor Hansen said "By recording your dreams and goals on paper, you set in motion the process of becoming the person you most want to be. Put your future in good hands – your own."[5] If all you do is think about your goals, you create no commitment to moving ahead to reach them.

As a sales person, I recommend you start every week by confirming where you are against your business goals for the month or quarter and the year. This allows you to do a progress check against where you should be and what you might have to either do more of, if you are on track, or differently if you are not getting the necessary results.

If You Think You Can, You Can
If You Think You Can't, You Are Right!

As Henry Ford said "I am looking for a lot of men who have an infinite capacity to not know what can't be done."[6] Many start so many tasks or projects or set goals they do not believe can be accomplished and really set themselves up for failure psychologically and philosophically even before they get going.

How many of you start something by saying "I will try" and not "I will do it"; simply by changing your language you can change your results! Remember the Star Wars movie when Yoda said "Do or Do Not – There is no TRY."[7] Your language does define your commitment and can affect your results!

A Goal Is Simply A Dream With A Deadline That You Control!

You have all probably heard the adage 'there is no magic in small dreams' but just dreaming is not enough. You have to make your dreams tangible and real by picking a date by which you will accomplish them, or the sad reality is that they will probably never be reached. You also have to have control over the outcome; dreaming you will win the lottery by the end of the month is not a goal.

After Steve Jobs died, tributes flowed in from all over the world and you heard words like visionary, dreamer, innovator and more. I will absolutely guarantee you that Steve Jobs set big goals and did everything possible to make them happen and as President Obama said "Jobs was brave enough to think differently, bold enough to believe he could change the world, and talented enough to do it."[8]

Key Accounts

WHAT IS A KEY ACCOUNT?

It is not the rule in every company but a large majority of them have an easily defined number of Key Accounts that represent a significant percentage of their overall revenue. These key accounts will be defined by individual companies or sales leaders typically based on revenue but some may be added because they are strategic as well. Regardless, because they are so important to the overall revenue, you have to be very methodical and specific in how you plan for each key account.

This is such a big deal that you have to be much more focused and precise in how key accounts are managed. A review of sales literature shows the typical definition of Account Management as *"the process of maximizing the return on your investment in a customer by defining and actioning appropriate plans that will enable you to build on the present and to manage the future."* I would go so far as to say the number one challenge to achieving your objectives with a customer is "too few face to face meetings." Given the importance of key accounts I consider it a Sales Leadership responsibility to drive and manage this from an overall corporate perspective and work diligently and regularly with your sales team to ensure these key accounts are properly identified, supported and managed.

EXPECTATIONS OF THE KEY ACCOUNT MANAGER

There are a few expectations every Sales Leader should have with respect to how key accounts are taken care of by the individual account or sales manager including,

1. Be the primary contact with the customer. Not the only contact but the key contact. As a key account, you should have a number of contacts in the customer organization and you should be or already have facilitated the development of relationships between departments like Operations, Engineering and Manufacturing with the appropriate members of the customer team.

2. Understand the customer's business, market needs and environment and know the decision makers. It is vital to your account planning that you know and document as much as possible about the customer. Most companies have Key Account Profiles and use some type of CRM but the key is to have this written somewhere other than the sales person's notebook or worse, in his or her head.

3. Develop a unique strategy and tactical plan for each account. One size does not fit all. You need to have SMART objectives (Specific, Measureable, Attainable, Realistic, Timely). More than that, you must have an individual plan that includes long term strategies as well as annual and quarterly tactics down to specific measureable activities. This also needs to be written down and tracked.

4. Continually add value to the overall relationship. The more you are able to move from being seen as a salesman to a trusted advisor, the stronger your business with this customer will become.

5. Identify new customer requirements and challenges that lead to opportunities. It is only by being close to an account and following through on all of the above that you can position yourself for this.

6. Act with integrity and professionalism at all times adhering to both your Company code of ethics and be mindful of the customer 'rules of engagement' as they relate to vendor relationships.

KEY ACCOUNT RELATIONSHIP CONTINUUM

As much as you would like to think that you have great relationships with all your key accounts, you need to do a short analysis and really figure out where you are in what I and many call the relationship continuum. It really does not matter what you think – it is critical to understand how the customer perceives your Company and the relationship. More importantly, what is the effect of that perception on how they respond to you and what you need to do to move further down the continuum.

My perspective is that the relationship continuum has four stages from commodity through supplier through value added supplier to technology advisor or partner. The closer your relationship is to being commodity based, the more likely it will be all about price. On the other hand, the more you move to the Technology Advisor/Partner type relationship, the less price is an issue and the stronger the loyalty the customer will have to your Company.

What is quite common when you offer a number of products and services is that individually each offering may be at a different part of the continuum. The strength of your relationship can go a very long way to slowing the downward transition to commodity and speed up your ability to get new products or technologies adopted that can reshape your overall business. Given this, one of our best tactics you can employ is to strengthen the relationship you have with the key decision influencers and makers in your customer organizations.

KEY ACCOUNT PLANNING STAGES AND PROCESS

There are four stages to actually completing individual or unique plans for each Key Account and they include the following

1. Account Strategy. Your strategy for each account needs to start with a clear understanding of the customer industry, current situation and 3-5 year objectives so you can determine what they might need from you to achieve those objectives. Let me reiterate this; your strategy for each account must be tailored. It is critical that you understand how you can add value for this specific customer. Once you have the strategy in place you can create SMART objectives that if fulfilled or completed will take you to your targets with this account.

2. Relationship Plan. To build a good relationship with an account, you need to have multiple relationships with all the key influencers and decision makers. Too often, account managers have one or two people they talk to in a key account and that just may not be enough, especially when major projects or initiatives come along and you have no connectivity to the real key decision makers or influencers. You must know their individual business agendas, how they are recognized and what you can do to support them. For larger accounts, you should build an org chart and map out who in your Company should be interfacing with who in the account.

3. Clarify and Identify their needs and wants. By having a strategy and relationship in place you can begin the process of looking for opportunities. For each of the SMART objectives previously outlined, you should create multiple specific actions or activities that will take you closer to achieving the overall objective.

4. Performance or Satisfaction Measurement. On completion of each project or transaction you must conduct a satisfaction review with the customer to ensure 'attaboys' are passed along, mistakes or errors are corrected and learned from and your understanding of how this customer buys and values your Company is enhanced.

109

SPECIFIC KEY ACCOUNT PLANNING TASKS

For each key account you have to do the following

1. Assign a specific revenue target. This should be based on a combination of buying history, known opportunities and identified potential spending.

2. Identify where the revenue is coming from in terms of what products, services or offering and when expected.

3. Is the expected customer spend based on one or more projects, upgrades or additions to existing installations or just normal course of business spending? Is it based on Operations and Maintenance budgeting that typically has easier spending processes, or is it Capital budget that is usually more involved? Additionally, what is their procurement strategy, ie RFP or tender based at one extreme or sole source directed or something in between?

4. Put in place a written tactical plan that includes

   a. Key contacts in the key account you plan to meet with and with what regularity.

   b. What specific business development activities will you commit to accomplishing in this account.

   c. Any special marketing or sales approaches you want to take with this account.

5. Ensure the plan and the activity is entered and maintained in your CRM.

If this is really a key account in your Territory, expect that the progress in executing your plan will be closely monitored and measured on a very regular basis by your Sales Leader.

SEE THE FINISH LINE

For each of your key accounts you must be able to see a clear path to the revenue target for the full fiscal year. That does not mean you have to have the revenue and backlog in place already but you should have confidence in your pipeline for this account. If you are currently struggling to identify where the revenue is coming from to meet a key account target, this is where you really need to do some very specific account planning with emphasis on targeted activity and actions that will create the visibility on the revenue that you need.

Metaphorically, this is a marathon and not a sprint. You need to train hard to start the marathon and you will find it very difficult to complete. You will hit the wall more than once but if you persevere to the point where you can actually see the finish line, it gets so much easier from that point. That is what you are trying to do here with your Key Account planning – get to where you can see the finish line and then it really is simply a matter of executing one step at a time.

MANAGING YOUR KEY ACCOUNT TIME FOR MAXIMUM RESULTS

This may seem a bit simplistic but a very effective way to determine how much time you should be spending in a key account is directly proportional to the relative expectation of revenue against total target. For example, if you have a total FY target of $2,000,000 and one of your key accounts is expected to generate $200,000 in revenue, then you should be spending approximately 8-10% of your time or a half day per week working in and on that account.

This time should be allocated against three specific weekly actions

1. Brief review each week of status of the account and current opportunities to plan next steps that fall into one of two specific actions, either

2. Regular face to face meetings to advance current opportunities and identify new business, or

3. Follow up actions both with the account and internally to ensure opportunities are advancing, solutions are being developed and quotes/proposals, etcetera are being completed as needed.

What you have to avoid is getting caught spending hours working on accounts that are not generating enough revenue to substantiate the effort. In particular, you must be able to hand off non key accounts to Inside Sales to manage on your behalf.

GET INSIDE THE CUSTOMER DECISION CYCLE

To position your Company to win business in a proactive and managed way, you need to make sure you are meeting often enough with key accounts, that you have the chance to influence their spending. At every meeting you must reinforce your value proposition. What you also have to do is gain an understanding of their issues or problems and work to be able to provide solution options well ahead of any procurement decision. This means knowing, at a minimum,

1. The decision makers. Having relationships with the technical staff and other influencers is good but nothing beats having a direct relationship with the person who authorizes the purchase.
2. The project budget. Without an approved budget, there will not likely be an order unless it is an operational emergency or other exigent circumstances exist.
3. The Timelines. When are they making the decision, when do they need delivery and/or installation? What is the urgency?

What you are really talking about here is making sure you have the relationships to be able to have an engaging and meaningful dialogue with a customer. When you leave their office you want them to say something like "that was time well spent – I always get value from meeting with those people". This will give you the ability to get ahead of their decisions and influence their spending.

Team Player

WHAT IS A TEAM PLAYER?

According to Wikipedia, '*Teamwork* is the capability to comprehend and recognize the diverse strengths and abilities in a group setting and then applying them to one final solution."[9] The concept has spread from the world of sports where it is well known and accepted, to business, so much so that it is in danger of being considered by some as an empty buzzword, or a form of corporate-speak. In the 21st century, as people are becoming more sophisticated and society is becoming more technically advanced, working as a team makes it easier to accomplish goals. Some things cannot be accomplished by people working individually. Larger and more ambitious goals usually require that people work together with other people. Anyone who has ever been to a job interview will invariably be asked what the concept of teamwork means to them. This is because companies today want people who are team players, people who are able to get along with their colleagues and work together in a cohesive group. Because teamwork is the oft-desired goal of many organizations today, they will often go to the effort of coordinating team building events in an attempt to get people to work as a team rather than as individuals.

It is not just good enough that you are all in the same metaphorical boat but you all have to have your oars in the water and you have to be pulling together. Your perspective may be different, your reasons for doing something may be different but at the core if you are all truly trying to accomplish the same things you will find convergence at some point. In the Army we had a fun phrase we used when we realized we were arguing but agreeing; we said we were 'in Violent Agreement'. Sometimes you just have to look at things differently to see more clearly. It is your willingness to do that, to change and adapt and to try to find common ground that creates a real team environment.

At the heart of this is your ability to communicate, to understand and where necessary to compromise even if only slightly, to ensure the interests of the Company are being met. It can be tough sometimes but the Company must come first; the adage 'Service before Self' rings very true.

To an Outside Sales Team it is very easy to feel very alone sometimes. You are out at the cold face of reality dealing with customers eye to eye, belly to belly and toe to toe and it is not always fun but that is who you are and what you do. Never forget that behind you is a Team of individuals who are committed to the overall success of the Company. The more you keep them in the loop and informed about what you are doing, the better they will be able to assist when needed.

WHAT DOES IT MEAN TO BE ON A TEAM!

To me, there are four key elements you need to demonstrate to truly be part of a team including,

1. Belief. You have to believe that what you are trying to accomplish is both realistic and achievable and your individual efforts will contribute to your collective success.

2. Trust. You must have trust in your coworkers, in particular when you handoff something for someone else to take care of for you.

3. Respect. This is key to enabling true collaboration, cooperation and teamwork.

4. Recognition. It is amazing how huge an impact this can have on people. It costs you nothing and earns you everything but it must be deserved and it must be sincere.

COMMUNICATE AND COMPROMISE

Communication is multi-faceted; it includes how well you present your thoughts, ideas and messages but it also includes how well you listen and accept what others have to say. You do not have to agree but you do have to work hard to understand what others are actually saying. You also have to understand their often unique perspective.

I have always told the people I work for and work with that I hate the idea of the "yes" man. I find contrarian views quite refreshing as long as they are well articulated and professionally presented. Like most, I do not like to be criticized or marginalized.

Do not tell me what you think I want to hear, but rather tell me what I need to hear. You may sometimes appear close minded with entrenched positions but when you present compelling reasons to strengthen and support your viewpoint or perspective, others are obliged to at least hear you out. This is the essence of good communication and offers opportunities for reflection and compromise.

Good team players pride themselves on being able to communicate effectively and acknowledge there are often better ways to do something than they might have initially believed, even if that forces them to change a mindset or an opinion or a way of doing things that has been in place for a very long time.

SERVICE BEFORE SELF

This is a strong phrase that has many connotations. Let me tell you what it means to me and you can decide for yourself what it means to you. I spent the first thirteen years of my adult life with my watch running five minutes fast; I was an Army guy and it was a huge 'faux pas' to be late for anything. More importantly and what some may have difficulty understanding, is that my Service came even before my own family. As an example, I spent three years in Germany and in the middle of the night we could be called out to deploy and we had no idea if it was for real or an exercise and when or if we would come home. When I left the Regular Forces I took off my watch and have not worn one since. I still believe it is wrong to be late for anything but symbolically and philosophically I do not live the way I used to; at a higher level my family now comes before my career.

Does that mean my Company comes second? Not at all, but it means there is a time and place and my priorities are determined by what I am doing and when I am doing it. As a minimum, I have a commitment to my Company every working day. It also means that the business decisions I take must be based on what is best for the Company.

Time alone is not a measure of commitment or service. The real keys are your attitude, your willingness to engage, your resolve to get the job done, your unbridled support to your co-workers and your effectiveness in maintaining open and useful communications. You cannot be a team player if you do not believe and act in this manner. You cannot turn this on and off when it suits you; you either are committed to the success of the Company or you are not.

THERE IS NO 'I' IN TEAM
BUT THERE IS AN M AND AN E FOR ME!

Unfortunately I have heard this far too often as people try to rationalize why they do not work well in a team environment. As individualistic as sales types are, you must realize that to be truly successful you have to work in the larger Company Team. If you are at crossed purposes with Company objectives or philosophies, you only create confusion and delay.

Most real sales professionals are driven to maximize their bonus or commission income and will very often believe their interests and the interests of the organization are in conflict when it really is all about perspective. In my view, true success can only be achieved when your personal objectives and interests are in harmony with those of the organization. If you start from this point and recognize everyone is trying to meet the same overall targets, you will be in a much better place.

IT TAKES A VILLAGE TO RAISE A CHILD

I do not know who first said this but it is so true. No matter how good you are and no matter how hard you work, you can never be everywhere all the time and do everything yourself. You need to depend on others and the sooner you learn to trust them to fulfill their roles and responsibilities, the sooner you will be able to surpass all your expectations.

The message here is very simple; focus on your job and get better at it each and every time you do it and hand off all the rest to the organization to help and support you.

ONE PLUS ONE DOES NOT EQUAL TWO

I am a firm believer that the synergistic effect comes into play when two or more people with common vision and purpose work together to achieve an objective. They can create momentum and results that appear to be much more than what they could have accomplished individually. They can literally 'feed' off each other, inspiring and multiplying their efforts. This can only be done in a team environment with collaboration, cooperation and communications.

UNITED YOU STAND!

There is no question that, as a united team, you can accomplish whatever you set out to do. I cannot stress enough the importance of doing everything you can to work through any differences you may have with other people and get on a common path to your individual and collective objectives.

This is not about having a group hug. It is about respecting individual contributions even when you might disagree with an approach or recommendation. Work through the issues professionally and arrive at a consensus everyone around the table can work with. Maybe you have heard the adage that 'the best is the enemy of the good.'[10] What this says is that in your efforts to be perfect or the best, you often stomp over what are good and acceptable courses of action.

Sales Basics

DEATH OF A SALESPERSON

Simply stated, Death of a Salesperson is having Nobody New to Talk To! The reality of Sales is that you are either going up or you are going down; there is no standing still. The second you stop moving new people through the 'Process' is the second you start going down. It really does not matter that you have ten really good prospects at various stages of the buying process; what really matters is that you keep adding new ones into the funnel. I have seen this countless times; too many salespeople will say that they are just too busy shepherding their contacts through the process. They tell you they have no time to add new ones, so when the ones in the funnel either buy, stall or die off their sales grind to a halt.

To counter this you need to set aside time each and every day to work at adding new contacts into your funnel process. Another way of describing this is THE NAME OF THE GAME IS NAMES. Some of you are probably thinking that it is your Company's responsibility to generate new leads and there is some truth to that but you still should each have a long list of companies, departments and organizations that you can call to try to find new opportunities. Remember that old Sales maxim "If it is to be, it is up to me."

CAN YOU HAVE FUN WITH REJECTION?

This is the second biggest killer of Sales! Rejection can be really tough to handle. You invest a lot of time, energy and even money into a prospect only to have them not buy at all or buy from someone else and it can hurt. It is okay to 'grieve', but not for a day or an hour; maybe for a minute or two. Shake it off and get on with it. Remember the SW4 mnemonic that stands for Some Will, Some Won't, So What, Someone's Waiting or NEXT!

What you really need to do is work out your numbers. This is a simplification but it will illustrate my point. If you know that for every three people you start in the process, 1 will have a definable opportunity and for every three opportunities, 1 will ultimately buy, that means for every nine you start with you will make one sale. Let's say that each sale is worth $27,000. So you line up your nine prospects and starting with the first you ask "will you buy?" and they say no, so you move to #2 and they say no and so on down the line. Finally you get to #9 and he or she says yes. Woo hoo – you just made a $27,000 sale. Who made you the most revenue? Trick question you have probably already figured out, but I will explain my math anyway; if you divide $27,000 by nine prospects, each prospect is really worth $3,000 to you. If you follow that through then you made $24,000 off the ones who said NO and only $3,000 from the one who said YES; you made more revenue off the NOs.

Some will say this is a silly way to look at your business but I can assure you this is exactly how most top earning professional salespeople think. Every NO moves them one step closer to a YES. They know their numbers and they know their averages. It may be different for your various buying groups (corporate versus government) or for your different product or service offerings but this is all track-able. I will never suggest that "if you throw enough mud at the wall some will stick" but what I am saying is that there are countless reasons why prospects will say NO; just accept it and move on.

The other key part of rejection is understanding when NO actually means NO. A good friend in Ottawa taught me years ago to ask "Is it NO for now or NO forever?" Salespeople who earn in excess of $250,000 per year know and understand that a prospect will say NO as many as four to six times before they say YES. Too many sales people hear the word NO and they put their tail between their legs and slink away never to go back to that prospect.

You have to have a way to measure your successes and failures. You have to know what works for you and what does not. This is not about what you say or do; it is about how you think and feel.

WHAT IS THE NUMBER ONE REASON SOMEONE WILL BUY FROM YOU?

I love asking this question in a room full of experienced sales people and hearing lots of different answers. Here are the most common ones I get
1. Because they trust me or like me,
2. Because we have great products,
3. Because we did a great job last time,
4. Because my Company has a great reputation

All of these are important considerations but they are not the #1 reason. It is really very simple – the #1 reason why someone will buy from you is because

YOU ASK THEM TO!

It always amazes me how many professional salespeople do not understand this. They work incredibly hard to move their prospects through the funnel, they spend weeks or months working the process, they do everything right and then they forget to ask for the order. Okay, there are lots of situations where you will get an order without explicitly asking for the business but if you have an expectation that your prospects will always do this you are sadly mistaken and destined for failure.

It all boils down to the simple fact that most salespeople are afraid to ask for the order because they do not want to be seen as a salesperson. Hmmm – need to think about that one a minute; sad but true. You do not need to have 42 different ways to ask the question; you just need to ask the question "will you buy from me today?" or whatever best fits your situation. You know the really ironic part is that most prospects expect you to ask for their business and are probably disappointed when you do not. They wonder "what did he not tell me, what am I missing here? If he is not asking for my business maybe there is something he is not comfy with."

Everyone reading this probably has dozens of quotes worth significant revenue floating around that have not turned into business; when you have a few minutes, call these people and ask for their business.

QUID PRO QUO (Something for Something)

You Sell - They Buy!

The perfect business relationship. You sell stuff to your customers and they pay for it. Simple and uncomplicated. Notice I wrote this as you sell and they buy and not they buy and you sell; the former suggests that you have to work for the business and the latter is more about waiting for the order. It spotlights the difference between a proactive and reactive sales strategy or a sales professional and an order taker; which are you?

When It Is Free How Much Value Does It Really Have?

Is it just me or are you suspicious of deals where FREE screams out at you? When I see furniture stores advertise you get a free TV with the purchase of a living room set do you really think the TV is free? All I am saying is that when you throw something into a deal for free up front, especially when working with even reasonably experienced or astute business customers, you are not likely going to get much of a positive reaction.

If you want to offer an item for less than full value, I would recommend you mark it down to actual cost instead of simply giving it away. When you do have to give something away as a 'quid quo pro' to your customer, be sure to show the line item cost as a real value and then under extended cost show the price as the reduced or zero cost to reflect that there really is a discount being applied.

If It Looks Too Good To Be True, It Probably Is!

The next thing a lot of sales people do other than giving something for FREE is to simply make the deal look so good that the customer really does have to wonder "what the heck are these guys up to? Is their business that bad they really need our money or is their product so bad they almost have to give it away because no one will pay full price or what?"

Be careful when you put together a quote because you do not want to leave the impression that you are desperate for the business. You want to create some desire on the part of the customer to want your solution and you need to structure the offer so it is compelling without being overdone.

Give A Little, Take A Lot!

You do not have to give away the proverbial farm to get the customer to come to your side. You simply need to be seen as accommodating or flexible in your negotiating to gauge the type of 'give' you have to offer to win the business. More importantly, you do not have to offer special discounts but rather you can offer one time incentives.

If you offer strong value to the customer you can always negotiate some of this value without discounting the actual sale. For example, if your goal is to sell hardware but you also offer services like installation or commissioning, you may want to reduce the services piece so you do not create a precedent for lowering your follow on orders for more hardware.

It Really Does Have To Be A Win – Win to Work!

No matter how badly you want the business and how openly and professionally you negotiate, at the end of the process it will only work out if it is a WIN - WIN proposition for both parties. That is the challenge, but the result will be sales success. In your negotiations you need to start by offering enough to get their attention but do not give away your position too early.

Know going in what your final position will be. You must be very clear where you might have to draw the final line, because if you do not have that in place you can get caught up in the process and make a bad deal. Remember that sometimes a NO can be a good thing if you maintain the integrity of your prices and services.

SALES NUMBERS RULES OF THUMB

There are a few numbers based rules of thumb that you need to be aware of, especially when trying to complete your time and activity planning. Over time you may be able to adjust these based on your own personal experiences but in general these are pretty representative.

The 3 To 1 Rule Is Alive And Well!

There are so many places where this is completely relevant but especially when you start looking at the complete sales process as follows,

1. It takes 3 'suspects' or contacts to create 1 good prospect.
2. It takes 3 good calls to get 1 appointment.
3. It takes 3 good appointments to get 1 good opportunity. What I mean here is you need to meet most new prospects more than once before they really start to open up and tell you about their problems and issues. It takes a relationship and that takes face to face time.
4. You need a pipeline that is 3 times the expected revenue to meet the target for the commission or bonus period you are working on, whether it is monthly or quarterly.

The 80/20 Rule

This is the one rule I really, really want to prove wrong because it says that 80% of your productivity will come from 20% of your team. Check your numbers and see how accurate this is on your Team. From a sales person perspective, the 80/20 Rule says that 80% of your territory revenue will come from 20% of your clients.

When you run the numbers in both cases, you may find yours to be different but it is quite likely that the majority will come from the minority. You have two jobs; reinforce the success you have in those key accounts and work hard to grow the revenue in the remainder of your accounts or new accounts to create better balance and be less dependent on the few.

The 70/20/10 Rule

I came up with this rule for my sales team a few years ago. Review your territory individual purchase orders and figure out what your average order size is. For example, if over a fiscal year you received 100 orders for a total of $2,000,000, then your average order is $20,000. This is your sweet spot and based on this.

1. Spend 70% of your time working to develop and close business ranging in value from $15,000-25,000 and turn all lower value opportunities over to Inside Sales if possible.
2. Spend 20% of your time working to develop and close the bigger deals worth greater than $100,000. You need these bigger orders to pull up your numbers but if you spend too much time on them and they do not close then you can easily miss your targets.
3. Spend 10% of your time planning, administering and reporting. This includes keeping track of what you handed off to Inside Sales or Sales Support to close and manage for you.

'X' Planned Sales Calls A Day!

As Sales Leader, you may define this number but you should plan to have your team complete a certain number of sales calls every day. This does not always refer to face to face meetings and can include a webinar or phone call, but to be classified as a good call you should be able to add real information to an existing opportunity or identify a new one. Making appointments and doing routine follow ups does not typically count and takes significant time and effort but if all you do is those types of customer interactions you may not really be moving ahead too well.

WHY ARE FACE TO FACE MEETINGS SO IMPORTANT?

In today's electronic world there are lots of people who believe you do not actually have to meet to accomplish anything, but I will admit I am not one of them. I met a fellow in a hotel in Toronto recently who leads an international sales team for a Fortune 500 subsidiary. This guy made my travel schedule look like I never left the office and when I asked him why someone as senior as he is with a very large team travels so much, it came down to a few words, namely 'out of sight = out of mind'!

He told me he had tried to reduce his travel schedule but the reality is that when he stops personally making calls on his best customers, they start doing business with his competitors. He owns the C level relationship and his team owns all the other same company relationships. If you are not top of mind when the customer is making a buying decision you can be easily overlooked or simply forgotten; sure you may get lots of little business but when it comes to major purchases you may be playing roulette with your revenue. When I asked him why he could maintain the relationship on the phone, he reminded me how much busy people see the phone as an interruption. The best way to prevent this is to focus on maintaining the relationship on both a professional and personal level through face to face meetings, activities and events.

The Critical First Meeting

There should be absolutely no question the first substantive conversation you have with a new prospect must be a face to face meeting. Especially if you use a Relationship Based Sales Model, you cannot build a relationship over the phone or via email. Really understanding your prospect means getting in front of them to evaluate their manner, their demeanour and their body language. By doing it where they work, you can also evaluate the environment they work in and perhaps even manage a tour of their facilities and possibly meet other people as well.

133

Your challenge in getting this meeting is to strike the fine balance between telling the prospect just enough to get the meeting and not too much that they think they can say "not interested" before you get a chance to meet.

The Problem Solving Meeting

There is an old maxim that you can deliver good news by any means possible but bad news should always be in person. The same holds true for how you should deal with challenges. At the first hint there might be a problem with an opportunity, an existing project or deliverable or the relationship in general, you have to get directly in front of your customer to work to solve the issue and move ahead.

It is never fun to receive news from the customer that there in issue, especially if it is significant. In those circumstances you have to be cautious to respond and not just react. If you do not know the situation and are only hearing about it for the first time, you should always acknowledge the issue and ask for time to investigate and work with the Company to put in place whatever remedial or corrective action is necessary, if any.

Where you have made a mistake that has caused a problem for your customer, I highly recommend you take ownership of the problem on behalf of your Company. Once you have worked internally to find the solution, you need to meet directly with the customer to explain how you will 'make it right'. More long term business relationships have been defined by how well problems are addressed; customers want to know you stand behind and support what you sell and deliver.

The Customer Satisfaction Meeting

Once you have completed a project with a customer you need to complete a customer satisfaction review and again, this is best accomplished face to face and depending on the size and scope of the project it may be a meeting involving a number of people. You must not be shy about doing these to garner feedback on what was done well and where you can make improvements the next time around. Where you know the customer is satisfied even before you conduct the satisfaction meeting, one of your key objectives should be to gain approval for a 'testimonial'. It might include diagrams or pictures that you can use on your website, in an application note or white paper or other marketing piece. You need to make a concerted effort to build up your portfolio of success stories you can use to help grow your business. And like any other meeting, this gives you an opportunity to ask about new business or referrals.

The Opportunity Development Meeting

This will likely be the most common meeting you have. This is the meeting you set up with an existing customer on a regular basis to either find new opportunities or sort out technical issues and requirements or they can simply be part of the normal follow up and follow through process. Unlike the other types of meetings that are all fairly structured, this meeting can take many forms depending on the specifics of the meeting. You could be doing a Technology Update to a group of sales and/or technical people. You could be doing a single technology detailed presentation to provide insight for a specific problem or requirement. You could be bringing Engineering or Product Management into a meeting to finalize your understanding of a specific requirement or you could simply be meeting with your customer for an engaging discussion on their upcoming priorities and projects.

When you bring technical assistance into your meetings, even if they are tied in virtually, you and this Sales, Engineering or Product Manager support need to agree on two things; who is going to say what and under what circumstances and who is documenting what. Especially if there are many people in the meeting, it is important you plan and almost role play how the meeting might go. This will ensure everyone will know who is taking the lead and how questions or issues will be handed off.

FIVE WAYS TO HAVE A GREAT MEETING

If you go to all the trouble to secure a meeting with a prospect or customer it is critically important that you have a great meeting and here are some thoughts on that subject.

Make A Great First Impression

You all know the old adage 'you only get one chance to make a first impression' and you know what – it is absolutely true! You need to make sure your first impression for every meeting, even with long standing customers, is not just okay but great. That means you have to be prepared, you have to have a plan and you have to have an agenda. That first impression starts the first time you connect with this prospect or customer, whether it is on the phone, via email or face to face. Avoid a couple of key pitfalls while working to create that great first impression, namely trying to sell too early and getting too technical.

Communicate With Unshakeable Confidence

Have you ever personally experienced or heard that a dog can smell fear? Well, confidence is sort of the same thing and your customers will be able to sense when you really do believe in the message you are delivering and have the confidence of your Company and your solutions. Would you buy from someone who does not exude that confidence and belief; I know I would not?

Make A Direct Connection Between Your Value Proposition And Your Customer's Industry Or Segment

What you are really doing here is connecting the dots between your prospect/customer's problem and a successful implementation of your solution, in a setting or environment that resonates with your customer. Telling a guy in the mining industry you have implemented many interoperability projects in the ambulance world may not get you any traction but telling the mining guy about what you just completed for one of his competitors could be a home run with one swing of the bat!!

No matter how enthusiastically you say "you can be the first" no customer really likes to hear that as much as "yes we have done that before and let me send you some specifics and a reference."

Set Action Items

You all know you should never end a meeting without agreeing to what is next but you would be surprised that far too many meetings end and there is no future plan in place. Especially if you are meeting with action or results oriented people, this will be easy to do as they are driven to move things ahead. Commitments need to be made including action items for completion and a date or time for the next meeting or follow up.

Make a Great Last Impression

You can do everything right and then blow it with a bad exit strategy. Remember that the first impression is very important but the last impression can be just that – lasting! Be careful of a couple things; be sure not to go longer than planned and do not be too 'gushing' in your thank you and goodbye comments.

Going overtime is easy to do and hard to recover from. You can try to mitigate the effect of going long by asking for permission to take some more time but it may leave the impression you cannot manage your time well. Too profuse of a thanks can leave the customer suspicious of your 'need' for their business. The key is to wrap up quickly and concisely, reiterate the action items and next steps, thank them for their time (and maybe business) and then leave.

GETTING THE APPOINTMENT

What If You Cannot Get The Appointment?

Hmmm, they are just really busy with projects and vacation is coming and kids are graduating and ....they really do like me and my Company.... OR maybe I do not have the relationship I thought I had! No, it is not that at all, hmmmm!! If you have a great relationship with someone you will get a call back or you will get an appointment, usually without too much difficulty. There will be times when it takes longer simply because the person you want to meet is really backed up but if this is a recurring theme you must re-evaluate the quality of the relationship as something is not as good as you thought.

What makes this even more challenging is that you cannot get the call back or appointment and you do not even know why. Until you get some traction you might never find out, so that means you have to change your tactics; here are three possible ways to break the stalemate.

1. OKAY OR GOOD – keep trying using the Persistence will Pay Off approach. You might even try sending a note or leaving a message that says something like "I am very concerned I have not been able to speak or meet with you and would appreciate the opportunity to understand the situation" or words to that effect.

2. BETTER – try to meet them at some type of offsite business networking activity or event that you know they participate in. Since you have a relationship you probably already know this sort of stuff.

3. BEST – try to get to your primary contact through someone else in the organization. You should have multiple contacts for each customer so now meet with one of them to try to learn what is going on without being too explicit. Once you are in the building it is a lot easier to manage a drop in to say hi or something to that effect. A little intelligence can go a long way to sorting out the situation.

You Need To Have A Long List

For many sales people, opening up doors in new customer organizations is one of the most challenging things they will do. You have to be prepared to deal with a lot of roadblocks; everything from not even knowing who to talk to through to getting past gatekeepers or getting call-backs to outright rejection. You must be thick skinned and persistent!

Like the rest of the selling process, you can never depend on a high appointment closing rate so the only way to ensure you get the number of new meetings needed is to ensure you start with a good long list of target companies and target individuals in those companies. This list needs to be a living document that is never very far from your reach. Sometimes as you are working on one thing, you will think about someone else you should talk to so pull out your list and add that company or name right away before you forget. Set aside some time every day or week to do some online research looking for target companies and have your list handy when you do this.

Finally, set aside specific time each and every day to make calls to set up appointments. Ignore incoming calls, ignore email and just focus on getting new appointments. At first it may seem like less than productive time but I will guarantee that if you lock in doing one hour of planned and targeted calls for setting appointments every working day for a month, your schedule is going to get very full very quickly.

It Pays To Do The Research

If you have to find a point of entry into a new customer organization, I recommend you take the time to do some research on the company and try to figure out who to target. My advice here is to start high and work your way down, so if you can get your initial appointment with an Executive and be referred from he or she into their team the rest is a whole lot simpler. In your research you need to try to learn as much as you can about what this company or organizations does, how it is structured and what is important

139

to them. If you can learn the name of a specific person to try to meet try to find out what you can about them from sites like LinkedIn or even Facebook; it is amazing how much is out there if you just look!

By having specific knowledge of their business and their own backgrounds you will be able to tailor and target your meeting message. Your success in getting the appointment will be highly improved if you come across as something other than a telemarketer or pitch man!

Build A Graphical Organizational Chart

Larger companies and government offices can be a nightmare to navigate. Understanding who does what and who reports to whom can make a huge difference in how you target new business. Many organizations protect this information but by asking lots of good questions you can usually figure it out.

You should have org charts developed for all your key customers and they should be updated often. For new customers this will be more of a work in progress but it is still a great support tool to your sales activities.

You Are Making A Sales Call So Be Practised And Prepared

I would even go so far as to write a script and practise it a few times. Do not just throw up a slide deck and then start regurgitating information, the so called 'Show up and Throw up approach'; rather work hard preparing both the presentation material and the messaging.

If you struggle to make these calls successfully, ask your manager or a co-worker who is good at them for assistance. You can also go online and search for 'making cold calls or making appointments' as there are lots of sites with great tips and techniques to assist you to prepare for these calls. Work through a number of these recommendations and see how they turn out for you and make minor adjustments as you work to improve at every step.

BACK TO BASICS

Sales is tough enough without making it even more over-complicated and once in a while you just need to simplify things. Here are some ideas on how and why to do just that.

Teachable And Coachable

Not all who read this are sports fans but I believe it is a pretty fair guess that most of you are, in one form or another for one sport or another. Have you noticed that even the very best at the top of their games have a coach or manager? Let's pick a few sports top performers and see if this is true.

1. Best Golfers in the World. Tiger Woods, Rory McIlroy, Jordan Speith - all have coaches.
2. Best Hockey Players – Alex Ovechkin and Sidney Crosby - both have coaches.
3. Best Baseball Player – guys like Mike Trout and Josh Donaldson are currently ranked very high and they have many coaches including the hitting coach, the fielding coach, the manager, etcetera.

I could go on and on but the message is the same. The very best in the world all have coaches and mentors and more importantly the very best are coachable and teachable. They work hard to improve themselves, they listen to the advice they are given and they stay open to fresh ideas. My question to you is simple; are you Coachable and Teachable?

Work On The Fundamentals

When I talk about fundamentals, I am talking about doing the little things really, really well. In Sales, that means things like setting and conducting appointments, doing follow ups, closing business and reporting your activities.

When was the last time you actually practised a call script before making the real call or did a rehearsal for a key presentation? I have been told by many professional sales people that is something only rookies need to do. Think about that for a minute and contrast it with the adage of 'practise makes perfect' and try to rationalize why you do not need to ever practise.

Repetition is The Mother Of Skill

This old adage is absolutely key to being successful. It is not good enough to try something once or twice and if it does not work for you to give up. It is only through doing tasks over and over and over again that you can truly get very good at performing them. There is no shortcut, there is no work around; the only way to become the best at what you do is to just keep working on improving each and every time.

Crawl, Walk, Run

When you go 'back to basics' you have to also take the time to get back up to full speed by ensuring that as you practise over and over again you do not try to go too far too fast. Going from a full stop to full speed (the zero to hero idea) is not a practical strategy for improvement. If you are working on doing a better job of making appointments with new possible customers, make sure after each call to do a quick review to figure out what went well and what went poorly and then make those minor adjustments that will make the next call better. As you get better at the calls and start to realize better results, you can start to lock down how you plan and conduct the calls and speed up how many you are able to make in a given time. After a few days or few weeks, this type of activity will become almost second nature and you can be at full speed.

FINDING HIDDEN REVENUE WITH EXISTING CUSTOMERS

Not too many realize it but statistics suggest it can cost four times as much to create a new customer than to create new sales with existing customers. For that reason alone, you should always be looking to expanding the revenue you have with your existing customer base through a series of planned strategic and tactical initiatives.

Cross Selling

Very simply, cross selling is expanding the number and quality of selling relationships between the key people in your Company and the customer organization and through these relationships making additional relevant solutions available. If you seem to be talking to the same people all the time and especially if the overall revenue with this customer is not growing, this may be an indicator that you are not doing enough to create these cross selling opportunities. Here is a simple three step process you can initiate now

1. Identify Cross Selling Opportunities. Guess what, it starts by making another list, this time of your key and best customers. On this list indicate specifically what solutions and/or products you have sold them in the past. It will be pretty obvious if there are gaps between what they have bought and what you offer.

2. What are the Key Characteristics of your Target Customers. Here, what you are doing is trying to figure out who has the greatest need and who might be in a position to buy quickly, even if just a small order to create credibility. How can you leverage the existing relationship, even if with a different person in the customer organization, to support your cross selling strategy?

3. Make an Action Plan. Like everything else, it is not just good enough to think and plan – you must EXECUTE to see results.

It is easy to believe you have already talked to all the people in a customer organization and know all those who make buying decisions for the types of solutions and technologies you offer but is that really true? People change jobs or leave, new people are hired, responsibilities change, new positions are created, etcetera and so there are lots of others you could be meeting and introducing to your offering and value proposition.

Up Selling

Very simply, up selling is increasing the value and profitability of an initial order by adding more or upgrading the products offered or by adding additional services, the so-called 'would you like to supersize your order today approach'. The key here is you are not trying to sell something they do not need just to increase your numbers. Rather, you are offering what they do need, even if they do not appreciate the added cost is really added value.

There is often reluctance to try to do this for concern or even fear that you may lose the initial order but if you truly know and understand your customer and their needs, then you are actually doing them a favour by up selling. Just tread cautiously here as it can backfire on you if done poorly.

Bringing Dormant Accounts Back To Life!

You probably have a number of accounts that have gone dormant on you. All you have to do is look at year over year revenues and it is very obvious where this has or is happening. The best and simplest way to bring dormant accounts back to life is to utilize cross selling strategies to identify new potential buyers within an organization or to offer new or different solutions that you not have sold in the past. You cannot simply keep trying to sell the same people the same things when they are not buying from you now, unless you are prepared to either take a significant margin cut or you find yourself lucky that only your technology meets their requirements.

The only way this is really going to happen is if you get into the organization and really come to understand what their key requirements and 'points of pain' are and offer solutions that help them overcome these challenges. In other words, you have to identify and present a strong value added business case that resonates with their decision makers; in the absence of such a proposition you are likely not going to bring that account back to life.

TIME MANAGEMENT

This is one of those subjects that can never be over emphasized and here are some thoughts on becoming better at it.

Once It Is Gone, It Is Gone Forever!

Just about everything you have that you can lose you can get back, especially anything material. You can even lose your love or your health and you can get them back. But time, once gone, is gone for good. How many times have you come out of a meeting or an event or something where your first thought or comment was "that was an hour of my life that is gone for good" so you all know what I am talking about here.

There are numerous courses and systems out there that you can use to assist you to manage your time but it is amazing to me how few people actually use these tools to any good effect. Maybe it is just because I am getting old, but I find I need the calendar and associated reminders on tools like Outlook and my Smartphone to keep me on track. I try to schedule all meetings and important phone calls so I can commit the time, prevent double booking and most importantly, ensure I am on time and prepared.

Ready, Fire, Aim!

Reread that thought again and ask yourself how many times a day or a week you might be guilty of starting something without having taken the time to plan and prepare appropriately. You have all probably heard the adage of 'going off half cocked' and it pretty much refers to the same thing. The message here is to take a few minutes to plan what you are going to do or what you are going to say. Simply by doing this you will become more efficient and more effective and perhaps most importantly, you will not have to redo something which is a huge waste of time and effort.

Time Spent On Reconnaissance Is Seldom Wasted

Military planning always includes what is called a time appreciation which, simply stated, is an analysis of the time available to plan and execute a mission. Always included in this process is time to conduct a reconnaissance, whether it be electronic or visual or on a map or a combination of some or all of these. So what does this have to do with Selling? Quite frankly, reconnaissance is all about gathering intelligence and in Sales that is a critical part of the overall account planning process. It can be time consuming and often boring but it will pay dividends long term.

It Is Hard to Drive Forward Looking Through The Rear View Mirror

You cannot dwell on the past. You can learn from it in an effort to improve your performance and results but what you should not do is waste a bunch of valuable time rehashing what is now behind you.

MAKING GREAT PRESENTATIONS

This is a fundamental skill for any sales professional so here are a few thoughts on this subject.

Always Be Prepared

The overwhelming majority of your presentations should be pre planned and structured but you must still be ready, with little or no notice, to give a presentation to a potential partner or prospect. I cannot count the number of times I have gone into a meeting intending to do one thing only to find myself having to do something completely different. Having taken the time to get the appointment, there is no way I want to defer this chance to the 'next' time.

Not All Presentations Are Formal

Quite often you will have to do a presentation in a very informal setting with no laptop, no screen, no whiteboard and maybe not even a great location but you still have to be able to deliver the message and advance the discussion to the next step. The best way to be able to do this is to be so comfortable and confident with your presentations that you can deliver them without needing to refer to them, at least the key points. Far too many people have to read from their own presentation material whether it is PowerPoint, flip chart, etcetera to stay on track. My advice is that you become expert at all your key message presentations.

Tell The Complete Story

It is important you tell your complete Company story at every chance. Sometimes customers need to hear the story many times before they really appreciate all the things you do really well. Even if your meeting is setup to discuss only one aspect of your business, you need to find a way to talk about all your core offerings, even if just while setting the stage.

Reinforce Your Value Proposition And Differentiators

Your Value Proposition should be the cornerstone of every conversation you have with your customers. You need to find ways to weave the message into every phone call, every meeting and every follow up. Remember what you are really doing is reinforcing from the customer perspective the two key questions of "what is in it for me" and "why should I buy from you." It can form the basis of your '30 second elevator pitch' as it should cause prospects to say something like "tell me more!"

A strong value proposition creates a differential between you and your competitors. This allows you to overcome possible objections including price and delivery. It is critically important the value proposition is completely understood and you need to have confidence in the message.

Make Each Presentation Unique To Each Customer

There are two key ways you can make each presentation unique

1. Create a formal title page for this customer with the name and date, especially when you use PowerPoint. Also, where possible, be sure to insert reference examples of success stories from verticals or companies that will resonate with your customer.

2. More importantly, in the discussion leading up to the presentation, try to ask good questions to identify some specific problems or issues you can focus on during your presentation. This can be done well ahead of time at an initial meeting or when you make the appointment or it can be done in the last couple minutes before you actually begin your presentation. While doing your presentation try to refer to these issues and show how you can overcome them to reinforce your Company's abilities and track record.

Good Questions And A Strong Follow Up Can Make The Difference

Even when you make an outstanding presentation and tell the whole story and focus on specific issues and problems this unique customer has, if you do not ask really good closing questions and then effect a really strong follow up, you may come up empty both in terms of opportunities and chances to revisit with this prospect again.

Finally, as part of your continuing efforts for self-improvement, master your presentation skills.

CREATE THE DEMAND

A lot of sales people go into customer meetings hoping to find an opportunity, whereas really great sales people go into meetings to create the opportunity. Here a few tips on how to do just that.

Tell Your Story At Every Chance

If you want people to buy from you, they have to know what you sell! Can you put your hand on your heart and state unequivocally that your customers know everything you offer? Do not take for granted that your customers know what you do, especially if your offering is evolving.

The other thing to be careful of is to prejudge what the person you are meeting with might or might not be interested in. Their focus may be closely aligned with only a small portion of what you offer but just before meeting you, they may have come from an internal meeting where one of their co-workers rambled on about struggling to find someone who could provide 'x'. It just so happens that you have 'x' and might get an instant referral. I have had this happen; the person I was meeting with stopped me mid-sentence, picked up the phone and called someone else to meet me.

The key is to get very good at hitting the highlights without taking too long. I will often just say something like "I am not sure if you or your team are interested in this or that but perhaps you can refer me to someone else in your Company that I could discuss this with?"

Strike While The Iron Is Hot!

When you are successful at creating an 'in' be sure to assertively follow up to ensure the initial interest does not fade away. You may have set a meeting to discuss a particular activity or opportunity and you or your customer do not have the time to discuss another opportunity, but do not just leave it alone until the customer raises this again. Over the years I have actually had many salespeople tell me things like "I will come back to that one after this one is done or I do not want to confuse my customer by trying to sell him on two things at the same time." That is really just a cop out!

Your job is to pursue each and every opportunity vigourously and with enthusiasm. Let the customer tell you to put one on hold but until or unless that happens you must continue to develop the business.

Ask Better Questions

One great way to identify interest is by telling your story. Another is with probing questions that get to the heart of a possible issue. Too many people ask weak questions and wonder why they cannot get any traction.

Let me give you an example of what I mean and for the example you sell specialized computer server hardware and ancillary equipment. "Since you operate your own server systems, do you need any uninterruptible power supplies?" Not sure how you feel about this but I think it is a pretty poor question because it is just too easy for the customer to say something like "no, we are good!" and the door is shut. Opening it again will take a lot of work. Instead, how about something like "Since you operate your own server systems, what would be the impact if one or more sites went down today without warning and without intelligently managed power backup?" Your customer could still answer with "no, we're good" but since you asked a very thoughtful and detailed question, it is more likely you will get a better answer that identifies if they have a solution already and who provides it and how it is working or you might just open the door to a 'tell me more'.

Steamroll The Competition

One problem you have when you create demand is you often open the door for your competition. Now you already know that you should not badmouth the competition, but you also want to try to slam the door in their face, so it is a very delicate balancing act. There are a number of different ways you can deal with competition and how you proceed will really be up to you based on your knowledge and experience with the specific customer.

1. When you are the incumbent, be careful not to appear too comfortable and do not presume the next sale is yours. Continue to work the customer relationship hard and if you ever get any idea you may not be doing absolutely everything correctly, work with the rest of your team to make things right. The best way to keep the competition out is to not give them a way to get in.

2. Rule one is do not bring up the competition first but if you are asked about it, I suggest rule two is don't directly slam or badmouth the competition but rather ask questions that might raise some doubt. This is a sales spin on the 'know thine enemy' adage which means you need to keep on top of what your competition is doing and how well they are doing it. For example, maybe you heard they were having problems with a recent project or installation and you could just say something like "I do not know a lot about them but I heard from Bill over at Company X that they were struggling on Project Y – have you heard that too" and leave it at that.

3. Be prepared to defend yourself and your Company at a moment's notice. Just like you will be planting seeds of doubt about your competition, the competition will be doing the same about you and sometimes it can get nasty. Outright misrepresentations, personal slurs and the like are not uncommon and you need to be prepared to deal with these. This is where other customer testimonials, discussions about your install base and leveraging your technology partners successes can all come in very handy.

Creating demand is a lot of work. It is so much more than doing a meeting and a follow up and expecting the phone to ring or fax to spit out a PO. It requires repeated visits to multiple people over time and it requires patience, tenacity and a long term commitment to success.

FOLLOW UP AND FOLLOW THROUGH

Assume your pipeline is quite healthy right now and you have more than enough projected revenue, even when factoring in the probabilities, that you will easily reach your target. This sounds crazy but it is not uncommon for a lot of sales people to ease up and coast for a while, instead of using this time to make sure you get the business and exceed targets.

Planned And Scheduled Follow Ups

Never finish a sales call without planning and scheduling the next call, which in effect is a follow up. Whether your action item is to produce a proposal or provide information or even if you have no specific actions, as the next step is really up to the customer, you still have to complete a strong follow up. Sometimes the follow up will be many weeks out simply because you and the customer have agreed there is nothing upcoming in the near future. Even in that situation a nicely worded follow up note to thank them for their time and to inform them you will follow up in 'x' weeks as agreed is a very good sales technique. When you are working to advance a current piece of business I would recommend the follow up be done in a timely manner. I prefer to mix up my follow ups with both phone calls and emails and in some circumstances will even schedule another face to face meeting depending on the customer and the situation.

Regardless of how you do it, you really must do good follow ups. Write them into your calendar, put them on your task list and be sure to do them with passion and determination. This is how you will improve the probabilities of closure and grow your business.

No Major Order Should Be A Surprise

There is no question that some opportunities can go from unqualified to qualified and to a PO in a matter of a couple days but that is usually the exception and not the rule. Most of the time Outside Sales has to conduct a number of planned sales calls and follow ups to advance opportunities through the process and incrementally over the timeline of your typical sales cycle. In the process, you will probably update each specific opportunity with new information and probabilities a number of times. When you finally receive the PO you should have already had the probability at 75% or higher depending on what system you use to track them.

The bottom line is that POs should be expected and this should be reflected in your CRM. The strength of your pipeline and the Sales Team confidence in the status of the opportunities will ultimately allow your Company to have predictable revenue. This in turn will drive resourcing everything from personnel to inventory.

Know Your Limit And Stay Within It!

I am borrowing this phrase as it makes my point, that as professional sales people, you have to be aware and sensitive to that very fine line between doing the right amount of timely follow ups and being seen by your customers as pushy. On the other hand all you really ask of your customers is they are honest with you about things like budget, timelines and decision making processes, so you can in turn work within their systems and boundaries.

THE FIVE C's TO SUCCESS

Commitment

Commitment = Doing what you said you would do long after the emotion you said it with has left you! It is very easy to get caught up in the moment and make a commitment only to find after time has passed and priorities have changed that the commitment is no longer really there. In your business, you need to maintain your commitment on two levels including,

1. Commitment to the Customer. It makes a huge difference to the customer when they know you are going to be there for them in the good and the not so good times. When you are able to show them you really are about more than the next PO and you really have their interests and concerns at heart, they are going to be much more willing to engage with you on a regular and ongoing basis. It is, however, a two way street and if the customer ultimately abuses you as merely a source of information or free technical advice and support and there is no commitment to a true business relationship, then you have no choice but to move on respectfully and professionally.

2. Commitment to the Company. This is equally important. It is more than just a willingness to put in the time and effort; it is also about embracing the processes in place and supporting the rest of the Corporate Team to not just win but deliver on your commitments to your customers. If you are truly committed to the short and long term success of the Company you cannot cherry pick which of these things you will be committed to; it really is all or nothing.

A few other thoughts about Commitment,

1. Commitment cannot be Conditional. You cannot only be committed if and when it suits you. I prefer to the use the word "when" versus "if" when faced with a situation with a customer. I have often been

asked to commit to starting a project even without a PO and I am very deliberate in saying to the customer "When I get the PO I will be more than ready to commit to the timelines and milestones as we have already discussed."

2. Just like you cannot be sort of pregnant, you cannot be sort of committed. You either are or you are not and telling someone you are committed is nowhere near as powerful as demonstrating you are committed. The adage 'Walk the Walk and not just Talk the Talk' specifically addresses this point.

Competent

What is interesting is that many of us tend to be very judgmental about the competency of someone else or the organization they belong to, based on a very specific experience or situation. When you present your Company to the outside world, you want to be sure you show your company core competencies but each and every person in the Company is not expected to be fully competent in all these things individually.

All companies have separate departments within which various individuals have distinct skills and experiences. It is not unreasonable to expect that each of these people must be competent in their responsibilities and not try to be everything to everyone in areas that are not their primary function or purview. For the Sales team you must first and foremost be completely competent in Selling. In your business, this also means you need to have a basic understanding and competency in the technology you offer but you do not have to be an Engineer designing solutions and you do not need to know all the intricacies about Operations. One of the challenges you face in Sales is that most people think selling is easy and anyone can do it, when in fact everyone knows the truth about that statement. As I learned a long time ago, Sales is the best paid hard work and the worst paid easy work someone will ever do!

My best advice is to continually challenge yourself to become better at what you do. Improve your core competency in your specific roles and responsibilities. Become better at setting appointments, be better at presentations, be better at follow ups and closing. Be better at sharing information using tools like the CRM, be better at building relationships and be better at adapting and adjusting to meet the challenges you face. If you can do this and do it well you will be a long way ahead on the road to success.

Capacity

This ties very closely to the previous thought of competency. As soon as you stray into areas outside your responsibility and especially when you are not as competent as the person who should be doing it, you immediately reduce your own capacity to do what you are good at and should be doing.

Capacity is all about getting absolutely the most you can out of your organization as a whole. This is where you have to work smarter and not harder. Most Sales people are Direct or Type A personalities. They tend to be impatient and when something does not happen as quickly as they think it should, they just jump in and do it themselves. What that does is reduce and not enhance your overall capacity. Most companies are always challenged with too few 'resources'. One of the challenges you have when many do other peoples work and it is not well tracked or documented is that it makes it very difficult to determine the actual workload, identify resource gaps and define the business case to fill the gaps.

The message here is to maximize your own capacity by working your roles and responsibilities to the best of your ability and have some trust that the rest of your Company team is doing the same.

Consistency

You all know the tale of the tortoise and the hare. Planned, methodical, determined and consistent effort will most often win the day. You need to be consistent in everything you do from making calls to conducting appointments to closing.

Have you heard of the idea of 'just one more'? Let's say you want to be able to do 25 push ups but you won't even try because you know you can only do 5 or 6 today. The idea of 'just one more' says do 5 today and then tomorrow do 6 or just one more and then the next day do 7 or just one more. Sometimes you may get stuck on a number for a few days until you get a breakthrough but you are not going backwards and you are not giving up. In Sales you can apply this to any number of things you work on daily, whether it is calls or follow ups or whatever. By applying the 'just one more' idea to the practise of consistency you are setting yourself up for accelerated growth and success.

Credibility

I have always said that the two things you never get back once lost are your time and your credibility. Making it even worse is that credibility can take a very long time to create but it can disappear in a flash. In Sales, you depend on being seen by your customers as credible and professional. They will judge you on everything you do with and for them. The best way to build your credibility is to be

1. Fully **Committed**
2. Totally **Competent**
3. Always **Consistent**, and
4. Working to your **Capacity**

THE SALE IS NOT OVER UNTIL …

The Paperwork Is Done

So what do I mean by paperwork? Some might think it is when the PO is received and entered. Some might say it is when the order is shipped and the invoice is printed and sent. Some might say it is when the bill is finally paid. Perhaps I am old school but to me the real key is getting paid because that is when the customer has told you they are satisfied with your product, your installation support and the any training you provided. That is when the sale is complete and you can move onto the next sale with this customer or another customer.

The Customer Is Completely Satisfied

Now I just said that when the customer pays the bill they must be satisfied but is that really true? Lots of Companies and people pay for things but really are not happy with what they got or bought. I recommend you always follow up with the customer after the invoice has been sent to complete some type of Satisfaction Review. The only way you can find out if the customer is really satisfied is when they tell you they are satisfied. Nothing short of them telling you directly in an email or on the phone will do the trick; you must get it straight from the customer to be valid.

It Is Over

Oh the word games I weave!! First of all, it was over when the customer paid and then it was over when the customer told you they were satisfied but in reality it may never be over. Many of your customers could be asking for long term support and maintenance commitments beyond the warranty period, so you tell me if it is really ever over. Depending on what you sell and especially if you sell systems or solutions, long after the customer has paid and long after the customer tells you they are fundamentally satisfied with their purchase, you may find you are still dealing with residual issues from that original sale. So to wrap this up, here is the startling revelation,

The Sale Is Never Over

Some of you might have seen this one coming so it is probably not much of a surprise. If you are truly doing your job of developing and building long term relationships with your customers, then you already know that the real key is not to get a single sale but to get many, many sales over many years. To put it in perspective, the transaction may be complete but the process of selling never ends.

Process And Prospecting

PROCESS MUST SERVE THE ORGANIZATION
NOT THE OTHER WAY AROUND

It would probably not surprise many of you that a lot of sales people actually see process as a hindrance to doing business and that is unfortunate. A well-defined and established process can make life incredibly simple, not just for the sales team, but for all the other people who the sales team depend on to be successful.

Where things go horribly wrong very quickly is when the organization basically serves the process rather than using the process to facilitate moving things along. This happens when senior leaders apply rigid and bureaucratic approaches to the process rather than understanding the process is a standardized way of doing things that might have to adapt and change to unique circumstances. For Sales, the fundamental things that must be addressed in the process include

1. A standard approach to how opportunity development flows from lead generation through to order fulfillment.
2. What are the trigger or action points that require sales leader review such as changing an opportunity to qualified status or changing probability of closing or approving quotes?
3. Who is responsible for what and how are the handoffs managed?
4. How is all this documented or tracked?
5. Who has authority to override the process?

A WEEK IN THE LIFE

Start Your Week And Your Day With A Plan

As you begin a new week, you need to take a few minutes to gather your thoughts and get organized after a weekend off. You should be taking the time to review your schedule and remind yourself of what key meetings and commitments for the week and the day await. You should also be reviewing any emails that may have come in since you shut down on Friday. Next you need to review your pipeline, as it should trigger a number of potential follow ups that need to be done right away. With that complete, you can now take a few minutes to determine your priorities, make a list of follow up meetings you need to set up and jot down a list of new contacts or customers you want to call on.

Set And Then Manage Your Priorities

As you begin each day you need to spend a couple minutes confirming your priorities for the day. These may include follow up meetings with customers, new meetings with new or existing customers to identify new opportunities and it may include some time to keep the CRM updated. Regardless, once you have established these priorities you need to get to work on them and not allow them to be interrupted by a ringing phone or incoming email. It is okay to let customer calls go to voice mail unless you were expecting the call. It is also okay to allow new emails to sit for a while until you have a break in your priority schedule.

Eye To Eye, Toe To Toe, Belly To Belly

Sales is a person to person business and the more personal you can make it the better. The phone is a useful tool but you need to get out of the office as much as possible and in front of your prospects and customers and this should take the majority of your average day, each and every day. Between driving time and meeting time you should be out of the office 75% of the time. Even accounting for travel time, by being organized and disciplined you should be able to complete no fewer than two and as many as five or six meetings a day, especially if you can group them geographically close together (including multiple meetings with different contacts from the same larger customer organization).

Where you cannot meet in person try to meet virtually if possible. Video teleconferencing and webinars are great tools to enhance the quality of a meeting and are substantially better than just voices over a phone or words in an email.

Coordination With Your Company

Every day you probably need to do some coordination with any number of different people in the Company to keep your opportunities moving forward. This daily coordination should not chew up a significant amount of time but rather is just one more thing that needs to be done regularly. For the most part it is the type of activity you can do when your other priorities are complete. In other words and in most cases, it should be a lower priority than your next customer meeting.

Feed The Machine

As you prepare to shut down for the week you need to make sure you finish by updating your CRM and taking the time to review your week and make a few notes to get yourself setup for the next week. When I say update the CRM, I do not just mean to update the higher level information but to also make sure you have added notes, updated Company profile information, closed those opportunities won or lost, added new opportunities as needed, etcetera.

You should have the CRM permanently open on your desktop and you should be working in it constantly and updating it on the fly. You should also end the week by confirming it is complete based on the activity you have done during the week. What that does is let you come back in next week ready to go and not starting the week playing catch up.

The other thing this does is what is often referred to as 'leaving tracks'. Good salespeople understand how critically important it is to provide this window on what they have been working on and what is developing. By providing this information and transparency to senior management, you typically dramatically reduce the number and frequency of opportunity or activity specific questions asked later.

DO YOU REALLY NEED TO PROSPECT?

Many sales people believe that prospecting is not their job and many think it is beneath them; just give them qualified leads and they will go out and sell! There is some truth to this, as prospecting is not selling, but when the reality that your pipeline is weak and your prospects of hitting your target are poor hits home, what other options do you have?

Large companies often have separate Marketing, Sales and Business Development teams and how they are structured and who they report to varies significantly. Typically, Marketing is responsible for advertising and lead generation activities, Business Development is responsible for creating new accounts and Sales is responsible for getting revenue. The lines can easily blur between Business Development and Sales but what should be very clear and unambiguous is that Prospecting is NOT a Marketing function.

I have always espoused that an unqualified lead, regardless of how it is created, is really just a Suspect. It is only after someone in Sales or Business Development has an engaging discussion with the Suspect that they can be promoted to a Prospect or what some would call a Qualified Lead or demoted as not worth pursuing.

My belief is that you should spend time each and every week on Prospecting to ensure the long term viability and success of your territory.

PROSPECT THROUGH MULTIPLE POINTS OF ENTRY

I am convinced one of the key reasons most companies are not meeting their growth objectives is because they are not talking to enough of the right people. You probably have great relationships with specific contacts in the majority of your key accounts, but the reality is that as long as you only depend on those few for your future you may well be self-limiting. Through those contacts you may continue to do some very good business but you are not likely going to grow the account substantially over the multi-year average unless there is a specific one time procurement program in place.

Birds Of A Feather Stick Together – Not Always A Good Thing

One of the greatest challenges you face each and every day is to get out of your proverbial 'comfort zone'. When it comes to prospecting or trying to create new entry points of contact into a customer organization, you tend to do the things and talk to the people you are most comfortable with, hence the Birds of a Feather adage. If you have always talked to technical types, you will almost always tend to want to talk to other technical people. What you need to do is try to identify different groups of people to talk to. Who do you know in Sales, who do you know in Procurement, and who do you know in Senior or Executive Management? Each of the people in those groups have problems they need help solving and maybe your solutions will not be the ones they need today but how will you or they know until you talk to them.

If you really believe you are getting ALL the right information on a company by only talking to people in a single department, you are sadly mistaken. The larger the company or organization, the more necessary it is to have many different contacts in different departments where they each have different responsibilities and authorities. Some of your contacts will simply be able to reinforce or validate what you learn elsewhere; they may have little to no buying authority or influence but they know what is going on. Some of them will help you navigate the organization, steering you away from those that can derail you and pointing you in the right direction.

When you think about how you are going to get those new contacts, be sure to think about talking to groups or departments you have not typically targeted. I believe you will be surprised at how many new opportunities you will discover.

Who Do You Know?

Now I know this is not new to any of you but it is such a critical question that needs to be asked in every meeting that it deserves to be repeated here. If you are at all serious about meeting new contacts in your existing customer organization, you just have to ask this question at every opportunity.

For the record I will always chase a referral with priority. One of the worst things that can happen is to not follow up on a referral in a timely fashion and in the process upset the person who gave you the referral. I would rather be able to go back to my original contact and thank him/her for the referral as it gives me a chance to ask for more!!

Prospecting does not have to be difficult but it does have to be done. Getting referrals is so much easier than doing cold calls. In many cases, asking this question can also lead you to referrals in other companies or organizations. As long as the person you are asking for the referrals understands you will continue to work with and service their requirements, they should be very open to giving referrals but do not expect them to be offered; you really will have to ask for them.

Unravel The Threads

Have you ever pulled on a loose thread and it never seems to stop until a button falls off or you open up a seam in your clothes? This is what I mean by this thought, only with respect to prospecting for new contacts in a company or organization. Very often when you sit in meetings, some will start talking about co-workers they interact with in their normal course of business. Sometimes when you ask a question they will say something like "that is not my responsibility – Larry takes care of that." Too many sales people tend to nod but fail to ask "what is Larry's job?" or even better "would you introduce me to Larry?" or even make a note that Larry's name was dropped for follow up later. It really is amazing how, with simple questioning skills and even better listening skills, you can begin to draw a complete organization chart or have the chance to meet lots of new contacts.

I cannot tell you why too few people fail to generate new contacts or leads, other than maybe they think they are being pushy or too much like salespeople when they ask those questions. Sorry to break it to you but guess what – you are in Sales and you are not just expected but rather required to ask these questions. And you know what is even more ironic is that the decision makers on the other side of the conversation expect you to ask them too!

Next time you meet with a contact or even have an engaging phone conversation with them see how many new contacts you can get. Gently pull on the threads that appear in conversations and see how far you can take them; you are trying to get a name, a job title, a contact number and an introduction.

POWER PROSPECTING – GO WHERE NO ONE HAS GONE BEFORE!

It is very common to have multiple customers from the same industry or vertical because over time you learn about the vertical, solve problems that may be specific to that vertical and then apply it across the vertical. If you have done well, the word will get out in the vertical that you are the 'go to guys' for this or that which can have a dramatic and positive impact on your business. If you really want to shake things up, go out and start prospecting in a new vertical market. This type of prospecting requires patience and a disciplined and structured strategy to be successful.

Do You Know What Your Ideal Customer Looks Like?

There is a philosophy that your first task before talking to anyone is determining what your 'ideal' customer looks like. Many years ago I was taught a simple way to put together your ideal customer profile as follows.

Make a list of your top customers and then make a list of your worst customers. From that list try to jot down four or five common attributes or characteristics about each of those groups. Include things like willingness to meet, pays their bills, value more important than price, etcetera. From your perspective decide which of the attributes is most important to you and rank them in order. By doing this you will find that customers that may seem to be really great might show a couple of issues when you bring the lists together. Even if a customer only appears on one of the two lists, take the time to honestly reflect on both the positive and negative characteristics of this customer to determine where they really stand. Next, work to determine which of your customers most strongly exhibit these attributes and you should quickly arrive at who your ideal customers are for continued growth.

Once you have developed your Ideal Customer Profile you should use this profile to compare against every prospect and every potential customer you encounter. If those you are meeting and talking to do not meet the key characteristics of the profile, you really have to ask yourself if this is worthy of your time and attention. Time wasted on tire kickers or prospects who are not really serious can have a significant negative impact on your business. Finding people who fit the profile will greatly enhance your ability to meet or exceed your targets.

Do Your Research

Armed with your ideal customer profile, your next step should be to roll up your sleeves and do some good old fashioned research. Start by putting together a list of companies in the vertical you may want to penetrate. Work through their public domain information to determine if, at least on paper, they appear to be a good candidate to talk to. Public domain is not just their website but look them up on the broader internet, look at corporate filings if public and even check the Better Business Bureau if necessary. Dig down a bit to determine what their head count is, is the local office head office or just a regional office, who the Leadership or Management Team is, what are their revenues and who are their customers, what is their reputation, etcetera?

Finding And Getting To The Right Person

Assuming your Marketing team or other efforts have not provided you with a point of entry, you now need to find someone to talk to. Based on what and who you typically sell to is a good starting point. I like to go back through the Management team they promote on their website; look them up on sites like LinkedIn and see if any of your front line contacts have a direct contact with one of them. It will not be unusual for you to find out that even if one of your personal contacts does not have a direct contact, it is quite likely they are only one more layer removed. Use your networking skills to get someone you know to provide you with an introduction or take a flyer and send an introductory note and see what happens. Just be careful and make sure whatever you do you do not look like a spammer or telemarketer using questionable tactics to try to get a response.

Be Prepared to Have Fun With Rejection!

Expect rejection; everything from non-returned emails and voicemails to outright 'not interested' terse responses. The best prospectors are usually pretty thick skinned! Prospecting will not immediately lead to POs but it should quite quickly show up in the number and quality of new opportunities being developed and created.

Walk A Mile In Your Prospect's Shoes

Far too often, sales people go through all the effort to get a meeting and then spend most of their time telling the prospect all about their company and products and wonder why they get the brush off. You need to change your approach and work to understand why this prospect would want to meet with you and focus entirely on that perspective. As you are presenting your company, they are probably thinking about their challenges and problems and unless you can help them connect a possible path to overcoming these issues you are not likely going to get very far.

Learn and practice being able to highlight in just a couple of minutes what your core capabilities are. Because you have done your homework, tell a short story about how you provided a solution for another company that might resonate with this company. Finish with something like "I do not know if this is of concern to you but I would welcome the opportunity to learn and better understand how you operate and determine if I can assist you to overcome any similar or related challenges."

Rather than just blurting out the product pitch, take the time to develop your own script and adapt it to your Prospect. As quickly as possible find common ground and immediately demonstrate to them that you can offer value for their time and you will be off to a great start.

UP YOUR PROSPECTING GAME – GO UP!

One of the most important aspects of selling is finding out who is making the buying decision and ensuring you do everything possible to meet and influence that individual. Just figuring out who the actual decision maker will be can often be quite the challenge, especially for larger customers with very complex organizations. Managers will often represent they have authority when in fact they are only influencers.

I know a lot of sales people who believe that once they have a contact into a company, they are done prospecting when in reality you are prospecting at the very least until you identify a real opportunity that you can go after. Many times that first contact is the wrong person and it takes real drive and patience to persevere until you strike your gold!

Why is this important; quite simply if you are not selling directly to the decision maker you are expecting someone else to make the sale for you. When it comes to Executives there are a number of factors and suggestions that will help you to better position yourself and your company for a successful business relationship. The only way I know of to get the correct answer about who is making the buying decision is to ask direct and specific questions like "who has the authority to make this buying decision?" You cannot assume, you cannot guess and you cannot expect that because someone did have that authority at some point in the past they have the authority now.

Securing The Meeting

Figuring out who the decision maker is does not always mean you are going to be able to get a meeting. It can be really helpful if you have a coach or supporter in the organization that is willing to work with you to make this happen. What it all comes down to is that you must have a compelling reason why that Executive should meet with you or you will not likely be successful. To identify what that compelling reason is you have to first determine what is really important to that Executive.

To get the meeting you also have to be able to deliver the message in the form and manner that they want to hear it. You may have to do some real homework to find out if this particular executive prefers email to a phone call, does he or she have a 'gatekeeper' that screens both email and phones and if so what will it take to get past the gatekeeper. Again, having an internal coach can make all this much simpler but if you do not have someone assisting you from the inside then you have to do this all yourself.

You must also be persistent in getting this meeting. If your first approach does not work, go back to the drawing board and come up with a new approach. The bottom line is that, if you can deliver a compelling message, you should be successful in securing the meeting.

Make An Impact

Now you have the appointment you have to make the best of it. Meetings with Executives are often shorter than you would like and so you must be completely prepared. What you really need to find out as you do your final preparation for the meeting is as much as possible about this executive's decision making style. Some key information to determine includes

1. Do they like to get the full detailed presentation or just a summary?
2. What presentation style do they prefer – PowerPoint, whiteboard or a prepared paper brief that is discussed?
3. Do you need to establish your personal credibility or has that already been done by your 'coach'?

Walking into the meeting knowing how this executive accepts information and makes decisions gives you a significant ability to create rapport and establish your credibility. Walking in 'cold' and trying to figure it out on the fly could find you out of time before you even get a chance start.

So You Had The Meeting – What Next?

One of the key things you have to do in completing your meeting, if you have not already been briefed on this by your internal coach, is to confirm how and when the executive wants the follow up to be handled. Some want to be followed up directly but it is very common for executives to turn over the follow up to someone else who has the responsibility to compile the final information for forwarding back to the executive for a decision. In a perfect world it would be your coach but it will very often be someone else who may be new to you or someone you have not specifically done any previous meetings or presentations to on this particular opportunity. Now the selling process begins anew, albeit with support from an executive.

The other thing you need to be aware of is that some executives may be prepared to make a decision on the spot so you need to be ready to address that eventuality. It would be most embarrassing to have the executive tell you he or she is ready to proceed and what is next and you do not have an answer. The key message is to be very well prepared and ready for any twist or turn that is thrown at you.

Closing

WHO ARE THE BEST CLOSERS?

Maybe a trick question but take a moment and think hard about who are the best closers, meaning they get you to give them what they want? Kids!! They do not ever take no for an answer, they find a way to get you to give in and they can be so darned cute or cantankerous or whatever it takes. Finally, you give them what they want or you compromise, which means they still get something.

If you cannot close as a salesperson, you either need to learn how to do it or find another job. One of the most fascinating things I have learned in Sales is that most sales people either really dislike or do not really know how to close deals. Some sales people are natural closers but the reality is most just stumble through it, almost embarrassed by what really is the whole reason for getting into Sales to begin with.

What Is The #1 Reason People Will Buy from You?

This is a very important question. If you ask 100 people in a room you will get answers like
1. Because I really like and trust the salesperson
2. Because I really like the product
3. Because I really like the price

These are the most common answers and each and every one of these can be fundamental to making a sale but the #1 reason why people buy from you is *BECAUSE YOU ASK THEM TO*!!

In the end, it really is as simple as that. Everything else you do in the process leads to that most important and critical question "Mr Customer, will you buy from me today?" All those other answers are on track and they are relevant but they are not the real reason. It is also amazing how seldom, when as a customer, I get asked to buy!!

How You Ask Is More Important Than What You Ask BUT You Must Ask

The more professionally you ask, the more likely you will get an honest and direct answer. What puts off potential customers really fast is when you come across as pushy or desperate or both. There is an old adage "you can say just about anything to a friend as long as you are smiling" and asking closing questions to a customer is pretty much the same.

What is really interesting is that professional buyers such as procurement agents fully expect sales people to ask 'closing' questions. I know when I make a major purchase, whether it is for business or personal use, I really want to work with a sales person who knows their stuff and evaluate them based not just on their product knowledge, presentation skills, etcetera but also on their closing skills. Having said that it is better to ask poorly than to not ask at all!

Timing The Ask Is Very Important

Knowing when to ask for the business is one of the things that makes closing an art form. Anyone can be taught to simply ask for the order but true sales professionals are always doing two very key things as they interact with their customers

1. They are constantly monitoring the 'conversation' to identify opportunities to ask for the order in a timely manner.
2. They will ask for the order in a number of different ways and a number of times, fully aware they will either be ignored or rejected multiple times before they gain traction.

Remember, sales is a process and not an event and since closing the business is part of the process; it too must not be seen or practised as a singular event.

THE ABCs OF SALES = ALWAYS BE CLOSING

For those of you that remember the movie Glengarry Glen Ross you will recall that Alec Baldwin made this the key message of his rather aggressive seven minute lecture to the sales team and as much as you might disagree with how Alec pushed this, the message itself is very valid. As sales professionals, you have to be constantly thinking about closing the sale because if you are not, then you are not selling to customers but rather just having conversations with other people.

Once Is Not Enough

Very seldom will a customer buy the first time you ask them to; you need to ask for the sale multiple times and in many different ways before you expect to get the order. I have read it a number of times in different sales books that the average top sales earner expects to be rejected by the same customer for the same basic order four to six times before they finally succeed. When they do get the order, it is not because they wore the customer down but rather because they did the job of answering the questions, overcoming the concerns or objections and proving to the customer there was true value in the transaction.

Use Test Closes To Evaluate The Customer's Buying Mood

As you work through the process with a potential customer it is never really too early to work to find out what the buying mood of the customer or organization really is or is not. Test closes are simply a series of questions that give you some indication of where this opportunity is really going. Most of you already ask many good test close questions when you ask things like
1. Do you have funding allocated for this project?
2. Do you have a timeframe by when this needs to be completed?

3. Who has the authority to make the final procurement decision?

These are very direct and leading questions but if you cannot get a straight answer to most of these you are not likely close to an order. Not only do these answers start to define where your customer is in the process, it helps you to determine if the opportunity is even real.

If you want to have some fun and get a sense of what it is like to be put through this as a customer, take an afternoon and go car shopping. Good car salespeople use test closes from the minute they greet you to determine if you are a real customer or simply a tire kicker or time waster. If you spend more than thirty minutes with a real professional, they will likely ask you 10-15 very open questions that, to the uninitiated, will appear to be very soft and conversational but to you should be very telling. Here are a few examples of what to listen for because how you answer tells a little bit about whether you are just looking or might be serious about making a purchase.

1. Is there any car in particular you might be interested in?
2. Have you ever owned a Ford or GM or Toyota before?
3. Any specific reason why you came to visit us today?
4. Are you looking for another vehicle or would you be trading in your current car?
5. I know you said you were not buying today but if you were would you prefer that in blue or red or would you prefer cloth or leather?
6. What do you think of the adaptive cruise control option?

Make Sure You Are Closing The Right Person

I cannot even guess how many times I have done an outstanding job of making the sale only to find the person I 'closed' does not have the authority to make the buying decision and may only have limited influence. Especially in bureaucratic organizations (public and private), customers will often inflate their own authority and you only find out when the promised order never materializes. This is why it is critically important to cultivate multiple relationships in a customer organization to dig into who really does

181

and does not have purchasing authority; innocent questions to multiple people will most often provide very valuable clues as to who can do what.

Remember To Thank Your Customer For Their Business

Never take an order or a customer for granted. A simple thank you goes a long way to maintaining the relationship that can lead to more sales. If you treat each sales as a unique transaction that ends with the order you are playing fast and loose with your sales future.

THE GYM BAG CLOSING TECHNIQUES

I used to enjoy presenting this very visual and prop based discussion on closing. I would bring with me onto the stage a gym bag full of items and walk the audience through four of the most common types of closing techniques. You can decide for yourself what works best for you but in succession I would pull out of the gym bag one item at a time.

The Hammer. You have experienced this type of closing firsthand; this is where the closer metaphorically keeps hitting you over the head until you give in and buy. Not a preferred option for me but it does work for many, although this type of selling is very transactional and not conducive to follow on sales.

The Skater. Next out of the bag is a pair of old hockey skates to symbolize the closer who just seems to skate or stickhandle around the question and try really hard to get you to volunteer to buy so it seems like your idea. This is a much lower pressure technique than the hammer but since it often does not ever really get to the question it is not terribly effective. It can be a good option for very soft test closing.

The Sword. Of course as a former Army Officer I have my own sword so I would pull it out of the bag and take it out of the scabbard. That alone was really fun and the sword is a metaphor for the closer who is elegantly combative, using the 'thrust and parry' approach to handling objections and moving the customer into a corner and pinning them down. This can be a very effective technique depending on the relationship you have with the customer.

The Pen. To really make my point, I simply pull a pen out of my pocket telling the audience that of course the pen is mightier than the sword and say to the customer something as simple as "here is the contract; can you just fill in the blanks and sign at the bottom" and I can get this order moving for you right away.

Dealing With Adversity

A GREAT ATTITUDE IS CRITICAL

It Does Not Matter How Many Times You Get Knocked Down, It Only Matters That You Get Up Again

The test of success is one's ability to deal with adversity, accept setbacks and still move on. Have no doubt that you will have bad days or even bad weeks but it is how you deal with them that will determine your real strength of character and your ability to ultimately succeed.

Smart People Learn From Their Mistakes
Really Smart People Learn From Others Mistakes!

Unfortunately and as you all know, the lessons of history tend to repeat themselves so that suggests this thought is not really valid. To reinforce this, I have learned that even when you point out potholes and pitfalls in the road to others, almost all of them need to fall into at least one before they believe you know what you are talking about. Some people are so stubborn about learning from others and following genuine advice that they remind us of the adage that 'you can lead a horse to water but you cannot make it drink'. I go further and suggest that even if you hold the horse's head under water it will drown before drinking, if it is not thirsty!!

So what kind of person are you? Do you accept advice or do you insist on the school of hard knocks and learn it all yourself? Do you read biographies and autobiographies or other self-help books or do you 'veg' in front of the TV every night?

If you really want to improve yourself, learn how to deal with adversity and be successful, then you need to follow this thought a bit more than perhaps you have before.

No One Can Insult Me Unless I Give Them My Permission[11]

This quote is attributed to Eleanor Roosevelt and the message here is that a great deal of the adversity you face comes from how you interpret other people's comments and opinions. You probably take way too much far too personally; especially as salespeople, you need to be a bit more 'thick' skinned. A bit of a twist, but I would like you to substitute Reject for Insult. Next time someone does not buy from you just think of this quote and you should feel better.

When You Stumble And Fall Down Make Sure You Land On Your Back Because If You Can Look Up You Can Get Up

No matter how much you did to avoid those potholes and pitfalls discussed earlier, you are still likely going to stumble or trip at some point on your road to success. Rather than landing flat on your face, philosophically of course, it is really important you do not give up.

You must give yourself every opportunity to bounce back and get back on track. From a sales perspective, the best way to do this is to have so much in your funnel and in the process that you can take the attitude that "now I know they are not going to buy from me I can focus on my other business and not waste any more time chasing my tail here". When it took him over 10,000 tries to get the light bulb to work Edison said; "I just figured out another way it will not work!"[12]

When The Going Gets Tough, The Tough Get Going

Need I say more? Okay, well here are another couple quotes that give the same message

Quitters never Win and Winners never Quit

Whiners never Win and Winners never Whine

The spoils go to the Conquerors!

COURAGE IN SALES

Holding Your Position With A Customer

How many of your customers' premises have you been to where they have signs posted 'sales by appointment only' or 'no soliciting' or when you go to the desk and ask for someone the first question is "do you have an appointment?" You live in a world where you are not seen in the highest light by many. Even some of your best customers really believe you are beholden to them and therefore they can dictate the terms and circumstances under which they will do business. One of your key responsibilities is to be the customer advocate back into your Company but the flip side of this is you are also your Company's advocate to the customer; some days it is a very fine line you walk as you work to gain trust, respect and win business.

It takes courage to stand up to a customer and it takes a certain measure of diplomacy and tact to either disagree with them or 'educate' them when they may not be correct in their thinking or presentation of who you are or what you offer. The key message here is you cannot simply agree with them and take their side in an effort to get a PO but rather you must be able to clearly articulate your value proposition, your competitive advantages and why they should do business with you. I teach sales people to understand "the Customer is always right – except when they are not" and have the ability to get that message across without damaging the relationship.

Do You Have The Courage To Fail?

Sales is about trial and error. Sales is about persevering in the face of adversity. Sales is about taking 'abuse' from customers. Sales is not easy and it takes a highly motivated and somewhat unique individual to succeed and thrive in this type of environment. Key descriptors like persistent and resilient are often used for great salespeople but I would add courageous to

187

the list because only outstanding sales professionals are willing to fail each and every time they go in front of a customer.

Are you planning to fail? NO. Are you prepared to fail? YES. Are you willing to learn from each and every failure to be better the next time? I HOPE SO. If you can face your fear and do it anyway you will be a better salesperson!

Don't Just Accept Change – Embrace It!

I am sure you have all heard the adage 'the only true constant is change[13]' but my favourite is 'change is inevitable – suffering is optional!' Seriously though, it does take courage to embrace change as a normal course of business. Of all the people in your Company, Sales is uniquely positioned to take advantage of change in a positive manner because you get to see it coming from your customers. What really makes a difference is not what you see but how you adapt and respond to it. Remember the definition of insanity is 'continuing to do the same things and expect things to change for the better'[14]. The reality is that if you continue to do things the same way as you did years or even months ago you will stagnate, become frustrated and fail to realize your full potential personally and professionally.

Become an agent of change; get in front and provide leadership to your Sales team in general and your Company specifically.

Don't Just Criticize – Offer Suggestions And Recommendations

It is so easy to sit back and whine or complain as the proverbial armchair quarterback who has never been there or done that! Most companies are not perfect and are experiencing significant change and need your help in making sure they are both on the right track and doing the right things versus just doing things right. If you have thoughts or ideas on how you can improve as an organization you should be willing to express them to your management group.

It takes courage to challenge the so called Status Quo; most people are by nature risk averse. For those of you old enough to remember the Ford commercials from the 80s, I used to tell my soldiers "Ford is not the only one with a good idea" which basically says everyone's perspective is valuable and deserves consideration as long as it is presented openly, honestly and without malice or self-interest at heart.

Face Your Fears And Do It Anyway!

Not sure how many of you have heard this one but 'a coward dies a thousand deaths; a brave man dies but once'.[15] Given my military background, I often joke my Mom wanted me to be a warrior but all she got was a worrier. Those of you who have really gotten to know me understand I can get quite worked up over how things might happen as I play everything out, including every possible option, in advance, but I will tell you I do not let that get in the way of what has to get done; sometimes it just takes me an extra few minutes to do it!

You cannot plan to be afraid and you cannot plan to be courageous. What you can do it force yourself each and every day to focus on the basics and do what has to be done. For any sales team, that means only working on activities that will lead to revenue or a sale; hand everything else off or set it aside.

MANAGING THE EMOTIONS OF THE PROCESS

Plan And Hope For The Best But Prepare For The Worst

Just when you think and expect you are going to get that next key meeting or order or something else positive, something quite unexpected happens. Good planning forces you to examine and work through the contingencies you may need to employ to get a customer or opportunity back on track. In doing so, you are also more mentally prepared to handle the curve balls that are thrown at you.

Work To Avoid Surprises

Some surprises are nice to get but more often than not a surprise in business is usually not a good thing. A good example of a bad surprise is quote or proposal or tender requests that show up without any prior knowledge the customer was even looking for a solution; in most cases you are starting from a position of weakness. You can expend huge resources, both time and real money, in responding to tenders and your odds of winning are lowered by not having prior visibility on the tender and not having had any chance to influence the process.

The quality of your relationships with your customers will be the single largest contributing factor in the number of 'bad' surprises you get. Strengthening your relationships will reduce the surprises and provide a much more stable emotional work environment for you and your Company.

Manage The Expectations

One of the toughest things you have to do in Sales is continually manage other's expectations and this includes not just your customers but your internal staff as well. The simplest way to do this is by maintaining effective communications and keeping everyone in the loop. The simplest way to do this is to use the CRM to keep track of meeting reports, phone calls, email threads linked to opportunities, and so on and so on. When you fail to properly manage expectations, you set the stage for all sorts of emotions that create stress and complicate the workplace.

Focus, Focus, Focus

If you have ever listened to a professional athlete interview, they almost always talk about having to 'stay in the moment' and 'maintain their focus'. This lesson is hard to learn but critical to master for those in professional sales. You need to be totally locked on to what it is you are trying to do; when you allow yourselves to get distracted you can very easily lose your focus and not perform at the optimum level needed to be successful.

When you lose focus and then try to recover or get into scramble mode or whatever you want to call it, you create stress which in turn makes the emotional highs higher and lows lower. With strong focus comes mental sharpness and a better control of the emotions in play.

Emotion And Motion Go Together
Control One And You Can Control The Other

One great way to slow down the emotional roller coaster is to simply slow down. When I was in the Army, I used to say we operated at two speeds, namely Stop and Panic. The first thing you should do when you Panic is STOP! What a lot of people do when things start to go off track is to speed up everything they do; they talk faster, they walk faster and they expect others to get their jobs done faster. All that extra motion brings more emotion into the equation which is not always a good thing. What I recommend you do when faced with a challenge is to simply stop and think about it and try to figure the best way to manage it to a resolution.

ONE STEP AHEAD

Get In Front Of Your Business

The most important thing you can do each and every week and each and every day is to start with a plan of what you need to accomplish to create the activity that will lead to meeting or exceeding your targets. When incoming emails or phone calls drive your priorities, you will effectively have lost control of your plan and your day. I am not suggesting you ignore your customers when they contact you but I am saying that, except in rare circumstances, you should not drop everything you are doing to take care of their ask or problem. Understand your customers' needs and put them into the appropriate priority; it may be they want a quote but do not need it for a week so you do not need to get it done right away. Stay out in front of your business by staying in control of your priorities and plan.

Be Responsive And Not Reactive

You do need to take action when customers call or email but they should not become your only or highest priority in most cases. What I recommend is you get into the habit of working through issues or requirements and then, in a planned and organized manner, respond. I do not recommend you get caught up in the moment and react. When you respond, you are in complete control and have also likely marshalled support and resources from your Company. When you react, you tend to be alone and without a lot of backing. Responding allows you to maintain control of your agenda and keeps you one step ahead in your business.

Playing Catch Up Is No Fun

Once you lose control of your daily plan and managing your priorities you are effectively in catch up mode and that can create a whole new series of challenges. The old adage 'haste makes waste' comes to mind and I am sure you have all seen examples where mistakes have been made in an effort to hurry up and get things done.

I am reminded of what Stephen Covey said about managing priorities[16]; you need to focus on working on things that are Important and Non-urgent to be most productive. Urgent and Important is what happens when you are playing catch up and all the non-important things need to be lower priority whether they are urgent or not. When you stay in control of your daily plan and schedule you will be one step ahead of your business.

Leader Or Follower?

When you are one step ahead in your business you are demonstrating leadership. Followers, by the very definition, are under someone else's control. Whether you are dealing with customers or even your own staff you must come across as being organized, credible, and collaborative and on top of what is going on. One sniff of panic or desperation will create doubt and concern in the minds of others.

The message is to step up and step out in front and demonstrate strong leadership in your business in your territory.

Stack The Deck In Your Favour

Not that you ever want anyone to think that selling has anything to do with gambling, but you do want to ensure that everything you do creates the situation where you are definitely in the driver's seat and first in line to be selected by your customer community to help them solve their challenges. It is hard to be first in line when you are not one step ahead of the competition and in some cases, the customer too. I would never suggest this is easy to do but it can be done by continually revisiting your daily plan and ensuring you complete the tasks and activities necessary.

FINISH STRONG

The Art Of The Possible

As you try to finish off a month or quarter that drives your commission or bonus, make sure you review the pipeline and look for opportunities where you have pretty much done everything you can and are waiting for the customer decision to issue the PO.

You need to ask your customers if they are going to be buying in the near future. Be open and honest and tell them when your fiscal period ends and that you have primed your vendors or manufacturing to support you to finish strong and you just want to know if this opportunity has the possibility of going to PO soon. If you really have a good relationship with these people, you will be pleasantly surprised at how many of them will work to help you knowing you will do the same for them next time.

Be Prepared For Last Minute Price Haggling!

How many times have you done everything right, the customer has indicated they are ready to buy and then at the last minute they hit you with a request for a price concession, bigger discount or special deal? Not fun and especially when they suggest this could be an all or nothing type situation. The best way to avoid this last minute 'negotiation' is to deal with it much sooner in the selling process.

Price can be an issue but not nearly as often as most think. Before you react to their request for better pricing, you need to determine how real this request is or are they just asking to see if you can do something for them to make them look better in the eyes of their bosses? Does this last minute negotiation have the potential to really affect this specific opportunity or the long term relationship? Is this a customer that is even deserving of special consideration? Be careful to give best pricing the first time someone buys from you to try to get them as your customer as they will expect and often demand similar pricing going forward. Instead, work to sell them on your full solutions capabilities and your overall value proposition. Not all business is good business so you need to make sure you stay focused on the right business.

Watch Out For The Competition

Be very mindful that, in almost everything you do, you have competitors and if they are doing their jobs they are also trying to close the same business in their favour. If you focus on what the competition does or does not do on price or performance, you are putting the competition in front of the customer rather than keeping them thinking about you and your Company. You must stay focused on ensuring your customers understand your value add, your differentiators and how your offering meets their requirements. In this way you effectively outsell and marginalize the competition without ever even alluding to them or acknowledging they exist.

It Ain't Over Till It's Over!

Some of you may be at the point where you have given up on the current fiscal period and are changing your focus to the next one but it is probably still too soon to do that. You may have more than enough revenue in your pipeline to make a final surge but just need to stay focused and in control and do what you can do to make that revenue happen.

In many cases, there is a direct relationship between company performance and company bonuses or profit sharing or whatever it is called in your organization. Remember that each extra dollar of business you contribute in the fiscal period can impact the bonus many non-sales people earn and that can make a difference when you ask them for assistance and support for your projects. If you truly are a team, you will always keep that perspective in front of any self-interests you might otherwise have. Remember what goes around comes around.

DEALING WITH THE VACATION BLUES

A couple times a year you run into the problem of vacation periods getting in the way of doing business, whether it is the Christmas holiday season or summer vacations. Here are some ideas to overcome the frustration that can occur when this happens.

Remember To Give Yourself A Break!

The old adage is 'all work and no play...' Make sure you plan to take some time off yourself to recharge and refresh.

Plot Your Key Customers Vacation Plans

If you have a good relationship with your key customers, make sure you ask them about their vacation plans. While you are having that conversation, be sure to ask them what priorities they have to clear off their desks before they take their vacation to try to determine the status or urgency of the opportunities you are working on with them. Simply by learning these two key things, you can better plan your own time and not get frustrated when you get unexpected 'out of office messages' or no feedback from voice and email touches.

And when you do chat with them before they leave, get them to pencil in a tentative face to face appointment for a few days after they get back and you will touch base later to confirm!

If About 20-25% Are Away At Any Given Time, Then 75-80% Are Still Working

Not everyone goes on vacation at the same time and most people only get two to three weeks off in the summer. The good news is this means that well over half and likely close to three quarters of your customers are working every day too. It may be more challenging to do group meetings and the customer internal process can slow due to others being away, but you should still be able to have good direct updates with your customers.

There are two really good times to be very opportunity focused. The first is early in the new calendar year when it is either a new fiscal year for many enterprise organizations or for Canadian government agencies it is close to their end March fiscal year. In both, you have great reasons to sit down with your customers to figure out what is in the new budget or has to be spent right away. The other key time is early September and it is close to the end of the American fiscal year or only a couple months before the end of the calendar year. Many customers suddenly realize they have a lot to get done in the 90 days before the Holiday Season kicks in, so use these meetings to try to figure out what their priorities to finish their year will be and how you can help them spend their remaining budget.

Create And Maintain A Sense Of Urgency

Either you control your environment or it controls you. I could probably write up a list of 15-20 excuses why it is more difficult to do business during holiday seasons or I can simply ignore the excuses and get on with what has to be accomplished. The easiest way to keep motivated and excited about your business, even in the middle of the so called 'summer doldrums' or 'winter blues', is to maintain a sense of urgency to find new opportunities and close more business.

Ramp Up Your New Account Discovery Work

When your customers are on vacation, this is an ideal time to ramp up the number of calls you are making to work to create new customers and open new accounts. Many of them are going to be on vacation too but if you have a good list of contacts to call for that critical initial appointment you should be able to fill your calendar by making enough calls.

CREATING AND SUSTAINING MOMENTEM

It Is Much Easier To Slow Down Than Speed Up!

Sales is a marathon, not a sprint! If you have ever been a distance runner, you know how difficult it is to speed up once you are into the run but it is quite simple to slow down a bit if you are too far ahead of the rest of your Company supporting you.

Keep Your Eyes On The Prize!

Be very focused on what it is you are working to accomplish and go straight for that goal with no course corrections or deviations. When you are going straight at your target with strong momentum, any obstacles that you come across are much easier breached. When you start making sudden turns or even worse yet, start going in circles, you lose all your forward momentum and simply spin out of control.

Success Breeds Success!

There is nothing like success to really overcome adversity and sustain momentum. When things are going really well and you get into the proverbial 'groove' they just seem to keep going. It reminds me of the old adage 'that it is so much easier to work from Inspiration than Desperation'.

First, though, you have to create the momentum and to do that you absolutely must focus on doing the basics each and every day. Make and conduct great face to face appointments, identify new opportunities, get assistance to develop your solution, proposals and quotes and then go close the business.

HALF FULL OR HALF EMPTY?

Optimist Or Pessimist?

So you are in a bit of a slump and your numbers suggest you are
going to miss targets and maybe miss your bonus. Simply looking at the
numbers it would be very easy to be frustrated and down, however here are
three things I would like you to focus on including
1. Take the attitude now that the next 60 days are like a 'do-over' and
   load up on appointments to move business ahead.
2. Revisit your pipeline and figure out what might be the easiest
   opportunity to close even if it is fairly small. The key is to get a win
   and then build on that.
3. Never forget how powerful your perspective and attitude can be on
   your overall performance.

Self-Reflection Is Worthwhile

Every once in a while you need to sit down and spend the time to
reflect on what you have or have not done to achieve your targets. This can
be very difficult to do as you are not only asking the tough questions but you
really have to answer them as well. Human nature suggests you typically
want to assign or deflect any blame away from yourselves to others. It takes
a lot to look in the mirror and not shirk from accepting responsibility and
being accountable. For those of you that believe the glass is half full, you will
look at this as a highly important and hopefully productive activity that will
help you make the necessary course corrections to get back on track.

What should not be in dispute is the need for something to change or
to get better. Some things you are probably doing very well; the key is to
figure out what those are and do more of them. If, on the other hand, self-
reflection determines you need to change or get better in some areas, then
find a coach or mentor to work with and support you in this effort.

The Rising Tide Will Carry All Ships To The Top

Perhaps you are not really sure whether the glass is half full or half empty; maybe you are in the middle of a slump and so it is challenging to be positive. My advice is to look very carefully at your existing opportunities and select a couple where you have very good relationships with the customer and focus on getting a couple of small wins right away. Use the 'get back to basics' approach and use it where your probabilities are higher and allow these couple of wins to turn the momentum or the 'tide' back in your favour. With that in place, let this old adage begin to work for you and visualize the water getting higher and higher in the glass.

Be A Great Example

WORK LIFE BALANCE

A Break Is Often As Good As A Change

Every once in a while you need to remind yourself that you really do need to take time off. At one point where I was between positions, I was off for exactly two calendar months and I had really no idea of how much different I would feel with a break and a change like that. I played 52 rounds of golf, I travelled to Edmonton on Army Reserve duty three times and I had a great family 'vacation'. This was a combination break and change but a couple years ago to celebrate our 30th anniversary my wife and I took a full two week cruise and what a difference it made to go away for longer than an extended weekend or week!

Work Hard, Play Hard

No one is expected to put in 10-12 hour days and work weekends on a regular basis, but every once in a while this is just the way it has to be to get the job done. You cannot be in professional sales and plan to work a standard 8-5 day and just walk away at the end of the day until the next morning. Whether it is the time change you face as a company, travel demands, proposal or bid deadlines or simply customers who work 'goofy' hours and call you, all these things work against you having routine and predictable hours.

When you work hard and finally get a chance to blow off some steam, do so with equal passion and drive. Find a way to disconnect completely from work and learn to relax. Let's just admit and accept that really successful sales people also tend to be really Type A or Direct personalities who have no idea how to even relax but give it a try and you may be surprised at yourself!

Blackberry Or Crackberry!

It started with Blackberry but all smartphones can now be totally integrated into your Company system and that makes this technology totally pervasive and in many cases intrusive into your personal life. If you are the Sales Leader, you need to set and manage expectations, but the sooner you can wean yourself off your work device after hours, the better it will be for you and your team. There may be times when you have to take care of things regardless of the day or time but do not create a culture where people are expected to be able to respond at all times for what could be deferred until the next working day.

Your Customers Do Not Own You!

There is a huge difference between being responsive and being a 'slave' to your customers. They need to be respectful of the relationship and it is up to you to set the parameters. I believe the customer is always right, except when they are wrong! When the customer says Jump, you should not be saying How High but rather should be asking good questions about what it is they really want. When or if the customer decides to vent or proverbially 'tear a strip', sometimes you just have to grin and bear it and sometimes you have to gently but forcefully push back.

You can adopt one of two attitudes when it comes to a customer

1. You do what you have to do to win business and be successful, or
2. You do what you have to do to not lose business or the account.

The second option is totally defensive and as long as you are in that mode you are probably out of control and on the verge of heading into a downhill spiral. You should always take the attitude and perspective that what you offer is of significant benefit to the customer. If you cannot make them see and want that, then you need to move on. This will create a lot less stress for you, which in turn has a substantial impact on how your overall day goes and how much you take 'home' with you later.

In my world, **YOU OWN THE CUSTOMER** – act like it!!!

If It Is Not Fun It Is Probably Not Worth Doing or
Do You Live To Work Or Work To Live?

Okay, so every moment of every day is not going to be fun. You may even go a few days without really having a lot of fun. Personally, I dread travel days but I love being face to face with customers. Even when they do not respond or react the way I want, I still really get a rush to be in front of the people whose decisions make such a difference to me personally and to the Company.

MOVING AHEAD WITH PURPOSE

Evolution And Not Revolution

In order to grow, most organizations need to change. Sometimes change comes first and sometimes it follows depending on the circumstances, but change is truly inevitable. As a Sales Leader you have to get in front of the changes and often will initiate many yourself. When possible, you should solicit the ideas and opinions of the members of your team and create an open and transparent discussion.

The other piece of advice I have on change is to make it as seamless as possible. Sometimes a major change is necessary but often small course corrections implemented incrementally will suffice. The bottom line is that your team must understand that there are changes coming and the sooner you and they embrace and support these changes, the sooner your team and greater Company will be able to move ahead.

Leadership Is Not About Democracy
You Get A Voice But Not A Vote!

A good leader will provide a framework to their team to offer their thoughts, ideas, suggestions and observations as you work your way through the process of implementing changes necessary to support long term growth. Failing to meet your growth objectives is probably not an option and it is critical that the whole team understand that a number of small changes now that get you on track for success and will prevent more significant changes later. At the end of the day, the person accountable for the results has the challenge of making the decision. You hope it will be based on consultation and advice but the reality of decision making is that you can never please everyone.

If given the opportunity, you need to provide your input, your suggestions and your ideas. Most good leaders will almost always consider your perspective as part of the process as long as it is based on what is best for the Company or the Customer. Sometimes they will do exactly as you recommend and sometimes they will not and that is just the way it is.

Yard By Yard It Is Hard, Inch By Inch It Is A Cinch[17]!

An old adage but it still works. Others include
How do you eat an elephant - one bite at a time,[18] or
A journey of a thousand miles begins with a single step![19]

The whole idea of Change Management is relatively young and it is really only in the last decade or two that it has really caught on as a formal discipline with certifications and credentials. The point here is that if you are going to move ahead with purpose, you should move ahead in a managed and structured way.

There Are Exceptions To Every Rule

I always get asked the question "what about this?" and as this thought suggests, there are exceptions to every rule and sometimes the exception almost becomes the rule! As you move ahead and roll out new or updated strategies, tactics and initiatives I encourage you to work with your leadership and your team to figure out what really works well and what might need adjusting.

I believe that 'the only true constant is change'. I do not believe in change for the sake of change but I do believe in constantly looking for ways to improve and grow. I also do not believe in the idea that 'one size fits all' and for that reason you cannot always force every situation to adapt to the policy, procedure or rule. Having said all this, I do not go looking for ways to break the rules or find ways to work around them.

If you do everything from the perspective of wanting to be part of the solution and not part of the problem, you are off to a great start.

A TRUE SALES PROFESSIONAL

There has always been an attitude in sales teams that results are the only thing that matters, to the point where 'sales absolves you of all sins'. With that in mind, I am going to examine what it really takes to be a true sales professional. These are not attributes or characteristics but rather indicators of performance that you can use to guide your behaviours.

Revenue Is Critical

You must be doing things that lead to orders or revenue. The more of your average work day you spend on those revenue generating activities, the better your overall performance against target should be. If you need to clean your office, do it outside your customer normal working hours. If you are reading this book during normal customer working hours, put it down until later and get on with selling. Sales really is about doing two things well; find someone to sell to and then sell to them. Anything else is not selling!

Margin Rules!

As critical as Revenue is, Margin is the fuel that the fires the Company engine. The two are inseparable and what you need to have is a plan to ensure both are healthy and growing. Your challenge will be to maintain your margins in the face of competition, price pressures and commoditization. You need to be expert at promoting your value proposition and delivering that value to your customers or the next order will come with another round of price haggling and margin erosion.

The Pipeline Or Funnel Is Your Future

The pipeline is your path to predictable revenue and growing the pipeline should always be a top priority. Put in place tools that allow you to measure your pipeline against your target and use the factors that make sense for your business to determine what is realistic and possible.

Productivity And Not Activity Is The Key To Success!

It is not good enough to just be busy, you need to be productive. The best way to ensure this is to focus on your job, your responsibilities and your accountabilities. As the Sales Manager, you should be quite disinterested in hearing how busy your team are doing things other people can and should be doing. Every hour they spend being busy on something someone else should be doing, is one hour they are not being productive in Sales. If they have done a really good handoff and are concerned that their opportunities are not advancing, that is the time to escalate to you for resolution.

Know Your Limit And Stay Within It!

I can remember way back in the late 80's when I first read the book 'What Colour is Your Parachute'[20] that gives advice on changing careers, resumes, interviews, etcetera. I distinctly recall one key point that you need to maximize your strengths but also know and limit exposure to your weaknesses. Nobody does everything well; everyone does some things very well and some things poorly. Your goal should be to understand what you are good at and do it really, really well and do not try to do things you do not do well. For a Sales Team, that means being a master of your craft and on a daily basis only doing those things that are your responsibility but do them very, very well.

Be A Team Player!

To me there are four key elements you need to be aware of including

1. Belief. You all have to believe that what you are trying to accomplish is both realistic and achievable and your individual efforts will contribute to your collective success.
2. Trust. You must have trust in each other, in particular when you handoff something for someone else to take care of.
3. Respect. This is key to enabling true collaboration, cooperation and teamwork.
4. Recognition. It is amazing how huge an impact this can have on people. It costs you nothing and earns you everything but it must be deserved and it must be sincere.

SPORTS SHORTS

March Madness

What if you could create the same type of excitement and attention on your business that the media creates around the US College basketball playoffs? Imagine if what you accomplished in the next month or your metaphorical March determined how you judge your year! Here is where your ability to manage your priorities and stay in focus is critical; in sports jargon this is not the time to 'drop the ball'. March Madness is all about results; the winners advance and the losers go home. I would go so far as to recommend that for your March, set aside all activities that will not lead to an order and concentrate solely on those actions that can lead to immediate results. Start your March by reviewing your Game Plan and then get to work executing on the meetings and calls that will drive the results you need.

Stay In The Moment

Every sports psychologist I have ever heard says this may be the most important advice they can give their athletes, whether amateur or professional. It only takes a momentary loss of focus and concentration to turn victory into defeat. You often hear athletes who have won talk about 'being in the zone' where they just cannot miss. Have you ever been in the zone in Sales; what did it look, feel and sound like? I know I have and it is a really cool place to be where you have passion, charisma and momentum and it can be contagious! Whether you are making calls to set appointments, conducting meetings or doing follow ups, get into and stay in the moment.

Nobody Remembers Who Came Second

A tough pill to swallow and normally associated with quotes like "we gave it our best" or "we had a good run but fell just short" but the reality is this is simply a way to rationalize for something other than being on top. You teach your kids "it does not matter if you win or lose but how you play the game" but that does not apply to professional sports or sales.

You cannot control results, so be careful how you define what coming first means or you might just be setting yourself up for failure. As far as I am concerned, winning means planning and executing on your sales plan. Winning means setting a personal best each and every time you are in front of a customer; make the best phone call or conduct the best meeting you have ever done. Do the best CRM update, do the best handoff to the Company; that is what winning means.

Back To Basics

At all levels of sport every good or great coach keeps their athletes focused on the fundamentals and constantly practising the basics, especially if they are struggling or in a slump. What I find both fascinating and disconcerting at the same time is the number of so called professional sales people who say they do not need to hear about the basics because that is boring or beneath them; pretty scary actually!

I recently met the President of a small company who has a bookshelf full of sales and management and personal development books. When I commented we have similar reading habits, he said he reads them regularly looking to find one or two 'nuggets' to reinforce his basic skills and abilities. What a great perspective and attitude! How many times do you see a sports headline about an elite athlete that is struggling that reads 'Back to Basics'...what a concept!

Just Do It![21] (Whatever IT Is)

Talk about a quote that is now part of our everyday language that simply resonates in pretty much everything we do. What this thought really says is Talk is Cheap and ACTIONS COUNT.

CREATE AND SUSTAIN MOMENTUM

P=MV
Momentum = Mass x Velocity

Since I have a Physics degree, I thought I would offer a simple formula that sort of tells it all. In my view, Mass is the sum total of your Pipeline, which is a combination of the number of opportunities and the value of those opportunities. Velocity is the pace that you are able to sustain on a day to day basis in creating and executing meetings, follow ups and generally conducting your day to day activities.

With this in mind, I would like you to do two things as you start your day and your week. First of all, take 15 minutes to review your current opportunities to ensure they are up to date and valid in terms of estimated revenue date and value and ask "what can I do today to advance this opportunity to closure." Secondly, review your schedule for today and ask yourself "what else can I do with my time today to find new opportunities?" By doing this each and every day and then executing on the answers you give yourself you can create momentum.

Smooth Out The Bumps In The Road

Using driving as a metaphor, you burn less gas and waste less energy if you can accelerate smoothly and then stay at speed. Constant starting and stopping is frustrating, stressful and wasteful and should be avoided when possible. When you look at your business and your activity, it is really important to get into a repeatable and sustainable rhythm.

In Sales, you often find yourself being pulled in many directions. You are the customer advocate to the Company, however you must still be in control of your priorities and responsible for your productivity. You should start the day and week by reviewing your pipeline and your schedule and ensuring you are driving towards your objectives without too many side trips, detours and stops along the way.

Just One More

One of the most difficult things to do is to go from standing still to full speed. More importantly it can be psychologically very challenging to even start a ramp up if you do not believe you can achieve it. Think about saying I want to be able to do 25 pushups a day within 30 days; most do not think it is even possible so they will not even give it a good go. However, what if you took the attitude that you could do 10 now and if all you do is JUST ONE MORE every second day then in 30 days you would be doing 25.

This is sort of a spin off the old adage that 'Yard by Yard it is Hard but Inch by Inch is a Cinch.' The key to creating momentum is to first overcome the inertia that has been created, by either not doing something or only doing a bit of it every day or so. Once you have overcome that inertia, it really is as simple as incrementally adding more and more. At some point you will look back and realize momentum has kicked in and appointments are easier to make, you are getting more meetings and more opportunities and more POs are coming in every day.

Reinforce Success

One of the most effective ways to create and sustain momentum is to leverage every good thing that happens to drive your business. If you were just able to book a really key meeting do not take a break and pat yourself on the back but rather immediately make the next call to make the next appointment. Think about sports – the team with momentum never calls the time out. Success begets success and taking a break or pause will only limit your ability to create momentum.

DARE TO DO SOMETHING DIFFERENT

You Version 2.0

Now work with me here; V2 is always better than V1! How can you expect your team to change if you are not prepared to change first? Tell your team you are committed to changing, even if the changes appear quite small. Over time the idea that change is good can become part of the team culture.

Teach, Don't Preach

Most are guilty of pontificating from their thrones; your commit should be to do a better job of communicating. Where necessary, provide the background, insight, framework or context that gives your team a better understanding of what is needed and why. If everyone takes this approach you can become a more effective and efficient organization more quickly reducing the 'back and forth' so often needed to get clarity.

You should always strive to provide quality information in a timely manner and professional fashion. You should all be willing to take that extra minute or two to ensure your expectations or questions or 'asks' are clearly articulated and understood. A couple extra words or sentences in an email might save three or four Reply Alls or a phone call.

The #1 tool for reviewing sales related information is the CRM. In the absence of good information, a strong sales leader will be relentless in tracking it down and getting it entered. The secret to hearing less from your boss is to spend more time keeping the CRM current; this is closest you will all get to a 'Mute Boss' button!

Ask, Don't Task

This is all about not what you say but how you say it. Your team knows you are the boss and you should not have to sound or appear autocratic; by asking you take a lot of pressure off everyone without lessening the importance of what needs to get done. For those that are not on your team, this will almost always produce better results.

Exception Based Management

As a Sales Leader, you may find that rather than spending a lot of time working through each of your Territories on an opportunity by opportunity basis, focus instead on what has changed, what is new, what is different and what are the issues. Implicit in this approach is that 'no news is good news' but by the same token you live and work in a very dynamic environment so no change for too long might create an exception. The types of exceptions you should be looking for and looking into will include

1. Significant change in estimated revenue amount or revenue date.
2. Quotes over 30/60/90 days. Quotes outstanding for months suggest the opportunity is not well defined or was quoted too soon.
3. Qualified opportunities that are not quoted within 60 or 90 days.
4. Unqualified opportunities that never seem to move ahead.

Obviously the core of the information you will review will come from the CRM and as you should have clearly reinforced in a number of ways, there can be no excuse for not keeping the CRM current.

How Can You Make A Difference Today?

At the end of the day it sure feels good when you can look back and realize that you made a difference today for a customer, for a co-worker or for the Company. Rather than do this as a look back and be able to say "yeah I did something really good today," why not set out each and every morning to accomplish this as a personal challenge?

Making a difference is not just about doing big things; very often it is simply doing lots of things really well and the sum total of that effort allows you to feel good about your day.

Elevate And Motivate

HARD WORK

Sales Is The Best Paid Hard Work And
The Worst Paid Easy Work You Will Ever Do!!

Sales is tough. You have to be thick skinned, you have to be persistent and you have to be willing to do what it takes to win the business and get the order. It is pretty simple to evaluate the success or failure of a salesperson. Someone who just goes through the motions but does not deliver orders is just not effective in a front line sales role.

Selling is all about having a problem to solve. It is not about selling a Product or Service. You have to be ok with hard work. It is absolutely critical to being successful and all the top people in most disciplines or departments got there as a direct result of a strong work ethic and a willingness to put in whatever effort is necessary to get the order.

Work Smarter And Not Just Harder!

Working hard does not necessarily mean working evenings and weekends. It does not mean you have to 'Live to Work'. What you have to learn how to do is take advantage of the tools and resources available to allow you to be more efficient and more effective. It is about being organized and able to prioritize your work. It is about having the discipline to take the time to really think through a situation so when you do actually start working you are absolutely on the right track with little risk of wasting time and effort. If you have a team you work with, it is about being able to get the most out of your team and taking advantage of their unique skills and abilities.

It is also about continually striving to improve. Too many people will say things like "I am going to do it much better next time" or "I can do it twice as fast." Great to hear everyone is so motivated and excited to get the job done but I would rather everyone simply said something like "tomorrow

I am going to try to do it 1% better." This does not seem like much but over the course of a couple months of doing just 1% better each and every day you can build up quite an improvement. Let's say you want to be able to do 50 pushups and today you can only do 10. Maybe tomorrow just try to do 11 and do that for a couple days then do 12 and do that for a couple days then do 'Just 1 More'. Within a few months you could be doing 50 just as planned!

The Harder You Work, The Luckier You Get!

There is another closely related adage that 'Luck is what happens when Preparation meets Opportunity.'[22] In some cases, salespeople will get lucky by being in the right place at the right time and something really positive just sort of falls on them but this is really a rarity. In most cases, you have to make your own luck by just continuing to do the little things each and every day and striving to always just get a little bit better along the way.

Many really believe that all you have to do to get the PO is make a couple calls, send a few notes, prepare a nice quote, maybe do a visit and take the client out to dinner or golfing. You know travelling is a perk!! No matter what, it has got to be much easier work than debugging a few thousand lines of code, right? Well maybe not easier or harder but different.

So, roll up your sleeves and get lucky... or was that get to work!

Busy People Get Things Done

When you absolutely need to get something done, do you not think of the busiest person as the best person to ask? I am not referring to the person who always complains of being too busy or makes comments about how much they have to get done; I am talking about the person everyone knows is the team workhorse who works hard and gets results. When you ask this person if they are busy they will say things like "no more than anyone else" or "everything is in hand or under control." They are also the type that are always looking for more challenges and more responsibility. Which kind of person are you?

Challenge Is The Fuel That Fires The Desire

An odd quirk of human nature, but many people need a challenge to really get going. Maybe it is the adrenaline rush that comes with being under pressure or maybe it is the thrill of the chase but whatever it is, if you are one of these types then make sure to create lots of small and fun challenges for yourself to boost your motivation and desire.

PERSONAL DEVELOPMENT

Constant And Never Ending Improvement[23]

True professionals totally believe in this concept and more importantly, they live it! It is not just about the obvious things like taking courses, reading books and doing online research. It is more about the subtleties like asking for advice, reviewing previous activities to find ways to get better and the like. There is an old adage that says 'for things to change, you have to change and for things to get better, you have to get better.'[24] Find a few minutes to reflect on what you can do to embrace this key Personal Development philosophy.

It Is Your Attitude And Not Your Aptitude That Determines Your Altitude

Just being smart or educated does not necessarily mean you are going to get ahead. There is a belief in many companies that 'Knowledge is Power' but I would suggest that only through the Application of Knowledge can you Create Power! Your attitude to your job and co-workers is so much more important, especially in a team oriented environment.

It is even more obvious when things are not going well, that shows what your true attitude really is. When you've had a great day, maybe closed a big account or something similar and then run headlong into a tough situation, you probably just take it in stride and set off to fix it. When you have already had a bad day, maybe have a headache and nothing seems to go right and then that next big high priority issue comes along, you will find that your attitude will be really tested! Under those difficult circumstances, it will be your ability to not point fingers or assess blame but rather simply nod or smile and get on with trying to fix the problem or correct the situation that will really set you apart from many others.

My Mom used to always say "if you don't have something nice to say then it would be better to not say anything at all." So as you go about your work today remember to work a little bit on yourself and your attitude and see if you notice the difference.

Can You Hit A Target You Cannot See??

Few people can tell me what they DO want, but almost all of them can tell me what they DO NOT want. Goal setting is a bit of an art form and takes time and effort to be really good at. Lots of people will read a book or see a speaker and be very motivated for a few days. It reminds me of the fun definition of commitment, which is doing what you said you would do, long after the emotion you said it with has worn off!

The sad reality is that too many people spend more time each year planning their two week vacation than they do setting and managing their goals, whether these be relationship, financial, career, athletic or whatever goals. Think about New Year's resolutions - they are really just goals and yet most people break them within a couple days, if they even set them at all.

Think about your business for a minute. You probably set annual, quarterly and monthly sales targets for each of your Territories or Divisions or Accounts. These targets could just as easily be called goals and they provide a focal point for you to work towards. On a weekly basis you review where you are with respect to meeting the targets or goals and make adjustments as necessary.

Taking that down a level, I would recommend to each of the members of any Sales Team to look at each week and each day as an opportunity to start fresh. Set some realistic and achievable goals for what you want to accomplish today or this week or this quarter. You can set the number of customer calls or contacts you want to have, how many quotes you finish and send out, how much business you want to close.

Set realistic and achievable goals, measure your progress to meeting those goals, make the necessary adjustments when you go off course and reward yourself when you accomplish your goals, then start all over again!

221

Save The Best For Last

Ah, human nature! When faced with a number of competing priorities, the overwhelming tendency is to do all the easy and fun things first and leave the tougher and less fun things until the end. That usually means that by the time you get to the last few you are tired, worn out, frustrated and generally not in the right mood or frame of mind to really take on these more pressing challenges. The result is you often finish with less than ideal work or solutions, if you even finish at all.

My advice is that you get into the routine of looking at your workload and tackling the tougher items first to get them done and out of the way. Later, when your day is almost done, the easier or more fun items tend to keep your attention and focus and you get through them more quickly and with fewer delays. Your overall productivity and efficiency will go up and you will leave the day with a much stronger feeling of accomplishment.

An old but very good book I highly recommend is Stephen Covey's "The 7 Habits of Highly Successful People."[16] He puts into very readable and easy to follow terms a number of ideas and perspectives that you can immediately implement into your own daily routine.

Success Is A State Of Mind

There is no magic formula to becoming successful as it is really up to the individual to determine what success means to them. Society has its own set of labels and measurements to decide if you are successful but I do not recommend you get caught in that trap. You may be very successful financially but be miserable in your personal life, so are you really successful? You need to take the time to figure out what really has to happen for you to be able to call yourself successful and be secure enough to not let peer or societal pressure take you off your chosen course. I recommend a book from Napoleon Hill called "Think and Grow Rich."[25] Unfortunately, too many people I know subscribe to the philosophy of Sleep and Grow Rich!!

WHEN THE GOING GETS TOUGH

Focus On The Fundamentals

When things are not going well, the most important thing you can do is get totally focused on doing your very best at the simple fundamentals. Too many people make the critical mistake of trying to make it all back in one attempt and that very often leads to complete disaster. Let me give you an example. I am a golf fan and turned on the TV on a Sunday afternoon just in time to watch the last group play the last hole at a PGA Tour event. A fellow who had never won before and took eight tries at the Qualification School to earn his playing privileges had a three stroke lead with one hole to play, an almost guaranteed win. He hit a terrible drive in the water left when he should have just aimed way right to begin with. From just over 200 yards to the green he went for the hero shot, hit a tree and left himself with only a punch back to the fairway. He finally hit the green in 5 (he had a penalty stroke for being in the water) and two putted for a triple bogey and instead of the win (for a cool $1,008,000, entry to the US Open the following week, the Masters next year and a full two year exemption on tour) he lost in a playoff.

The morale of the story is that when you just need to make something happen, stay controlled, stay focused, take your time and execute the fundamentals really, really well. In your world of sales, that really means to make more and better quality Targeted Sales Calls to increase the number of new opportunities, number of new quotes, increase the pipeline and increase the odds of meeting or exceeding your targets.

First Things First – Planning And Preparation Is Critical To Success

Plan meticulously and Execute flawlessly. Every plan will encounter hurdles but the effort of planning also prepares you for those inevitable eventualities. It takes time and it is takes effort to come up with a plan but you will find in both the short and the long term that effort is definitely worth the investment.

The Phone Is A Tool And Not A Crutch!

My personal belief is that too many sales people spend too much time on the phone and too little time in front of their customers. I was taught a very long time ago you cannot get a $10 haircut over the phone but some sales types think they can make a $10,000 or $100,000 sale without ever leaving their office. If I had my preference, Outside Sales would not be able to receive incoming calls; they would all go to voicemail so you would not have the distraction of having to deal with what Stephen Covey calls Non-urgent and Non-important interruptions that take you away from your primary focus.

If you are unable to get customers to take your calls, return your calls or allow you to come and visit that is another issue entirely. You need to find someone to coach you on how to work through any or all of those situations but that does not change the key that the phone is a tool to make appointments and in some cases to conduct follow ups.

Eye To Eye, Toe To Toe And Belly To Belly!

I cannot stress enough that the most powerful tool you have in your selling toolbox is you being in front of your customer. There is no substitute for the personal touch and interaction. If that means you have to be on the road with overnights away from home a few nights a month that is part of what you have to do in Sales.

The ABC Of Selling – Always Be Closing!

You are in Sales. You are expected to ask for the order. You are expected to ask for the order multiple times. You are supposed to be experts at trial closes and all the various techniques available to really find out if the customer is in a buying mood and ready to give you his or her business. This is not rocket science; it is Sales 101. You have all done this countless times; you just need to make sure you are doing it every day!

What Is Your Comfort Zone?

Believe it or not, Wikipedia actually has a small write up on this subject. It defines the Comfort Zone as "a behavioural state within which a person operates in an anxiety neutral condition using a limited set of behaviours to deliver a steady level of performance, usually without a sense of risk."[26]

It is a bit of a contradiction but an old adage I often use is 'any fool can be uncomfortable' but what that refers to is creature or physical comforts and not the mental discomfort that I refer to with this thought. As you work through the rest of your day or week, the best way to improve your performance and results is not by moving out of your comfort zone but rather by expanding it.

If It Was Easy Then Anyone Could Do It!

It does take a special person to become a very professional salesperson. If you review the statistics you will find that Sales Professionals always come out near the top of the income charts.

If you are in Sales and want to consistently earn a six figure income year over year, you have to get very good at what you do and you have to be prepared to deal with frustration, rejection, long days, nights away, etcetera. If you want to live a comfortable low stress life with little to no risk, then you better be prepared to accept a lower income and limited career opportunities. Now, it is not always about the money but if you are one of those highly motivated by income, then maybe Sales is for you, but only if you are prepared to be uncomfortable a lot of the time.

225

GETTING OUT OF THE STARTING BLOCKS

Be Ready To Go!

After any time off, even a weekend, it is really easy to get off to a slow start by not being ready to go first thing in the morning. Rather than being invigorated by time off, many people seem to need the couple hours or a morning to get back into the rhythm again. You let excuses like "my customers need time to catch up" or "it is the summer doldrums after all" determine how assertively and directly you address your business and that is simply a huge mistake you just cannot afford to make. My recommendation is you start your quarter, your week and your day by taking just a few minutes to review your targets, confirm the key meetings you need schedule and conduct and then just get on with the work.

A Good Start May Not Guarantee A Win
But A Bad Start Usually Means A Loss!

It is just so difficult to recover from a poor first contact or meeting or if your initial proposal was way off the mark in terms of pricing or delivery or even the core solution. You have to do everything you can to make sure you do everything to the best of your ability right from the beginning.

Procrastination Is Suicide On The Installment Plan[27]!

You have all heard the jokes about procrastination before but the truth is that procrastination is the easiest way to almost guarantee you will not achieve your targets. Make a decision and a commitment now to do what you need to do each and every day to give yourself the best chance possible of not just meeting but exceeding your targets. If you have control, you must exercise it; you cannot control how your customers will act or react but you can control making the call and getting the appointment and conducting the best customer facing meeting you have ever done.

Keep Your Eyes On The Prize!

Maintain your focus, stay true to your goals and targets, do the right things each and every day to the best of your ability and you might be very surprised by the results you achieve.

CROSSING THE FINISH LINE

If You Do Not Make It To The Finish Line
You Can Never Be A Winner

In Sales, crossing the finish line is getting a straight and honest answer to the key question of "Will you buy from me today?" As you come down to the end of your fiscal period, it is imperative you determine whether your current opportunities will close, be delayed or be deleted.

Remember, getting an order should never be a surprise, so having done all the work to find and develop an opportunity you absolutely must get across the finish line. Be gracious both when you lose or win the business, but you must get that answer as soon as possible.

The Tortoise And The Hare

I am sure all of you have heard the story of the race between the tortoise and the hare. The lesson here is that it does not matter how fast or slow you move your opportunities along; what really matters is that you make it to the decision point at the end.

What I do not recommend is having no activity at all for a very long time and then have this big burst where everything is urgent. Sometimes this is driven by the customer but you have the job of managing the customer so it does come back to Sales. You must have the ability to manage your priorities and plans and allocate your personnel resources and these 'go all out at the last minute' things are unmanageable. This does not just apply to the Sales process but in fact applies all along by everyone in the Company.

There Are No Pictures On The Scorecard

This is a saying that comes from Golf. It really does not matter how you get the little white ball in the cup; the only thing that matters is how many strokes it takes to accomplish. In many ways I expect the same of sales people. I ask them to follow a process but I do not tell them how to do the actual customer interactions. You may have one poor meeting and yet still earn the business with a great recovery meeting the following week. You may hit a hole in one at your first meeting and walk away with an order or later the phone rings and you are given an order without having really done anything, but like golf these are considered 'lucky' shots and not the norm.

What is important is that you get the ball in the hole. You do not quit, you do not stop, you just keep moving the opportunities along to get to that key decision time when you either win or lose the business. Do your best at controlling the process, do your best to make every interaction count and do your best to finish strong.

In A Close Race Everything Matters

How many times has the final little effort made a huge difference in the outcome of the race? The lean for the tape or the reach for the wall will very often determine who wins and who comes second. In your business there is no prize for coming second; you win or you lose. You can take solace if you have the best technical solution or a better price point but unless you win the business the rest of it is simple rationalization when what you should be saying is I LOST and work to figure out how to WIN next time.

As you go about your day to day work with your customers and your opportunities, you must have the mindset, attitude and perspective that everything you do matters. You have to give 100% all the time; that little extra may make all the difference and allow you to say I WON!

Is A Win The End Of The Beginning or
The Beginning Of The End?

In sales, the ultimate goal is to earn the business and receive the PO. For the rest of the Company, getting the PO is the first many will even have any idea of this business. Sales must fully support the rest of the Company as is necessary to fully understand what is required and what the customer expectations are. They must also ensure the Terms and Conditions in the PO match what was agreed upon and quoted and there are no hidden side deals that could cause you grief later.

Additionally, delivering a successful solution or project or whatever to the Customer makes your next sales call that much simpler!

TECHNO TALK

Probe Problems, Don't Sell Stuff

In Sales, you need to spend the majority of your time on finding problems and not necessarily developing solutions or sourcing products or services. There is an old adage that says 'the bigger the problem you solve the more value you offer'. When you are meeting with your prospective customers, you should be much more focused on trying to learn as much as you can about the problems they have, than on trying to quickly find something for them to buy. The better you communicate the problem to the rest of your Company, the more quickly and effectively they can deliver a quality solution and proposal back to you for delivery to your customer.

Recognize Applications

Customers never like to be told they can be the first to try your product or service or solution. Especially if you are selling technology based items, you need to first understand three very critical things
1. What problem is the customer trying to solve?
2. How does the customer currently operate?
3. What is the customer's current infrastructure/architecture?
Once you have sorted out these things and based on a very good knowledge of what you have done for other customers in the past, you can start to identify potential applications and steer your conversation with your customer down that path to determine if there is some traction to move in that direction.

Sell The Sizzle, Not The Steak

This is not new but is definitely worth repeating. When you focus on the features and not the benefits you are getting into too much detail about the product or service or solution itself and not enough about what it can do for the customer.

Technique And Tactics Will Win Out In The Long Run!

From a purely Sales perspective, your ability to identify and understand customer problems by demonstrating strong selling techniques as part of a well-developed tactical sales plan will make a much greater contribution to your overall success than by pushing 'stuff'. As a metaphor, a lot of people suggest 'knowledge is power' but I completely disagree; the application of knowledge can create the potential for power but by itself knowledge is not tremendously useful.

To make my point, there are plenty of really smart, highly educated people out there who have menial low paying jobs. Selling is similar in that if all you do is spout chapter and verse about the 'stuff' you sell, in the absence of really understanding the problem and the operational construct of the customer, you are most likely doomed to failure.

High Tech, No Cheque

It is all about the benefits and not the features. It does not matter how low tech your product or service or solution is, the minute you focus on what it is and what it does and forget about what that means to the customer you may be setting yourself up for failure.

POWER OF P

Problems Are The Key To Finding Opportunities

To find new opportunities you must find out from your potential customers what problems they have and then determine whether you can help them to solve those problems. There is no magic here; it takes hard work to make the appointments and conduct the meetings. It is even more challenging to get prospects to open up in an engaging conversation where you can learn their existing systems, architecture and problems. With that information in hand, you can work with your team to develop solutions to overcome these problems with the goal to win and deliver the business.

Sales Is A Process And Not An Event!

Following process is fundamental to professional sales. Sure, there will be opportunities that fall in your lap but you still have to follow the process to turn those opportunities into revenue. Bluebird POs that are not in the pipeline are 'events' and you should be happy to fulfill them but that is not selling – it is order taking. Even your best customers have to constantly be sold to and to do this properly you must follow the process.

Great Presentations Are Critical

Every time you meet with a prospect or customer you must be able to do outstanding presentations on any and all of what you offer. Sometimes you will have a projector and screen, sometimes simply a notebook and glossy, but you must be able to tell your story, work to identify problems and focus the discussion on offerings and applications you can deliver. You have to be able to deliver your value proposition and company story anywhere and anytime.

You Must Be <u>Persistent</u>

Not every call or email results in a meeting and not every meeting results in an opportunity and not every opportunity results in a PO. You have to be thick skinned and persistent each and every day. Your strength of character is measured in the face of adversity. The bottom line is you can never, ever give up!

<u>Predictable</u> Revenue Is The Holy Grail Of Sales

Okay, in the end your real success is measured with real revenue and margin but your ability to plan and resource effectively comes from visibility on what revenue is coming next quarter and next year. It is only by having a robust and credible pipeline that you can properly manage risks associated with everything from increased staffing to ordering products for inventory. To have solid confidence in your Predictable Revenue stream you need a few key things including

1. Large backlog for delivery both in the current and future quarters.
2. Large qualified and high probability pipeline that goes out four to six quarters.
3. Tangible evidence of market potential for existing products and solutions for individual customers and vertical markets.
4. Each member of the sales team must have a full calendar of appointments for the current and following couple of weeks.

If you are Persistent in following the Process to complete a significant number of Presentations daily to identify Problems that lead to qualified opportunities, you will be well on the way to showing Predictability in your current and future revenue.

PEAK PERFORMANCE TIPS

Take A Break!

There is nothing like a good vacation. I joke about how it is only a good vacation if you spend too much, gain weight and come back to work exhausted. What time away does is allow you to clear your head, relax and enjoy some of the rewards and benefits your hard work has created.

Now be careful as there is a lot of truth to the view that most people spend more time planning their annual vacation than their personal and financial future, so practise some discipline and moderation to achieve balance in your life.

Oh, and when you do take a break, you are not expected to be doing work; do yourself and your family a favour and leave the smartphone off and the laptop out of sight. If you are like me and a bit 'work obsessed' at least try to limit yourself to just a few minutes a day to check on emails and calls. Even then, only deal with 'urgent matters' and pass them off to someone else to manage for you until you are back. Use the Out of Office feature in Outlook and change your voicemail to tell everyone you are away but make sure to have someone lined up to cover for you.

Stay Healthy And Fit!

If you are sick and tired of being sick and tired, you need to do something about it. Being healthy and being in shape can have a huge impact on your mental alertness, how you handle stress and how you get through a long day. I will admit that I seek comfort in junk food and that only makes it harder to meet my fitness objectives.

If you are not feeling well, call in sick; take a day to rest and get better. You are not doing yourself or your Company any favours by coming to work ill as you might affect your co-workers and you definitely will not be performing at the top of your game. You might say you can still do your job even if only at 80% but what if you are trying to close that key piece of business and need to be at 110%??

Be Prepared!

Whether you are going to do a face to face meeting or a key phone call, you need to take the time to be prepared. You need to review any history with this account or individual and you definitely need to start the meeting understanding exactly what you are trying to accomplish. By doing this you will maintain control of the situation and ensure you guide the call or meeting to the conclusion you are looking for. One of the challenges of taking unscheduled or unplanned calls is that the other person is really in control and you now need to carefully wrestle that control away.

Never expect meetings or calls to go exactly as planned, but the process of planning will also allow you to be able to make adjustments on the fly. Work through the possible scenarios or situations that might develop and you will be much more able to get things back on track if or when they go sideways.

If you are doing a conference call or multiple person meeting, sort out in advance who has the lead. Allow that person to hand off specific questions or issues to others as needed but once the question or issue has been addressed go back to the lead for continued guidance. There is nothing worse than appearing to be disorganized or worse yet, in disagreement when dealing with customers.

This individual or group planning does not have to take long; in most cases it will only take a couple minutes but it must be done.

Control Your Emotions!

When I talk about control it is all about knowing how to work with that particular customer. If they are the type that expresses no emotion, speaks very slowly and deliberately and only wants to talk about business, there is great risk in too much small talk or being too emotive. Remember all the lessons you have learned on matching and mirroring.

Losing control or worse yet, losing your temper, can be catastrophic to both that piece of business and that relationship. That does not mean you always have to agree with the customer; it just means you have to be able to express yourself or negotiate in a measured and controlled manner.

By being prepared for a meeting or call you also are better emotionally prepared, even if you anticipate the meeting will not deliver the results you are hoping for.

Eliminate Distractions!

There is an old adage that 'every distraction is equal' followed by 'a confused mind does nothing'. The best way to eliminate distractions is to remain totally focused on your daily and weekly plan and not allow that latest email or phone call to move you off track.

HALF DONE IS WELL BEGUN

Is The Glass Half Empty Or Half Full?

Take a few minutes to have a really good look at your results so far this fiscal year or period. Be brutally honest with yourself and realize that if you are not satisfied with them, it is important to recognize that you have the ability to make the next period much better. The critical first step in doing this is to be the Optimist that sees the glass as half full.

Secondly, you must take responsibility for what has or has not been accomplished; there are always contributing factors and external influencers over which you have no control but it is your Territory and your Target and if you want the credit and reward that come with success, you know the rest.

Thirdly, you need to turn these thoughts into actions by reviewing what you need to accomplish and resetting your plan on how you are going to get there. Finally, you have to execute your plan each and every day. As Napoleon Hill said "what the mind can see and believe, it can achieve."[25]

Over The Hump = Easier To Go Faster Downhill!

You always hear people talk about Wednesday as hump day; once you get through noon it is downhill all the way to the weekend! Philosophically, it is much easier to create speed and momentum going downhill than it is to slog your way uphill. Regardless of where you are in a fiscal period against your target, take the mindset that you are over the hump towards achieving your goal. What matters is what you start to do immediately to make the behavioural and habitual changes to get and stay on track. If you are ahead of target, take advantage of that to give you the confidence to have a breakout period. Always reinforce success and keep the proverbial 'pedal to the metal' and when you hit an obstacle do not allow it to slow you down long term.

In Like A Lamb, Out Like A Lion!

Some of you may not of heard of this adage but it refers to the month of March and winter; when March starts with great weather (lamb) it usually ends badly (lion) and vice versa. If you have pretty much had a lamb start to your fiscal period, it is now time to turn into lions. Get aggressive in executing your business plan, be ruthless in managing your daily sales calls and be the king of the Sales jungle.

It Does Not Matter How You Start
It Only Matters How You Finish!

If you are off to a less than spectacular start, you have to get over it and get on with it! You have the ability, the raw talent and the responsibility to put what did not happen behind you and restart with a new attitude and a renewed commitment to your plan.

There are literally hundreds, if not thousands of examples where the second half of a game, a school year, a business plan has been widely successful and totally overcame the shortfalls in place at the end of the first half. Now is the time for you to make it happen in your Territory.

SABER – A MNEMONIC ON THE CUTTING EDGE

S = Skills

There is a perspective to people not in Professional Sales that anybody can sell; all you have to do is smile lots, talk lots and pick up the tab most of the time. Unfortunately the overwhelming majority of sales people help to perpetuate that view, not by what they say but by what they actually do. If you look at the definition in Wikipedia, it is quite revealing that they say a Professional is "a person who is paid to undertake a specialized set of tasks and orchestrate them with uncommon skill."[26]

The message here is there are skills that need to not just be learned, but practiced and then updated on a continual basis. It is not just good enough to be a good presenter; you have to be great at presenting your Company story. It is not good enough to have great relationship building skills if you are not continually using those skills to grow the number and quality of relationships you have within existing customers and new customers. It is not good enough to know what your customers are planning to do; you must be able to effectively communicate that back to your Company via the CRM.

A = Attitude, Aptitude And Action

A great attitude is important but by itself is not enough. Aptitude is important but there are a lot of really bright or smart people who are not successful. Action is the key ingredient that makes it all work. You have all heard the adage 'Talk is Cheap' and you all need to move beyond just talking to actually doing. Your primary responsibility is to spend as much time as possible in front of customers – period. Your next most important responsibility is to document those customer facing meetings effectively. Everything else should be set aside or handed off to someone else to take care of; it really should be as simple as that.

B = Behaviours

This is a loaded one; most of you are probably parents and understand the challenges of modifying behaviours you deem inappropriate or unacceptable and reinforcing and strengthening the positive and good behaviours. Sales persons behaviours are typically dictated by their compensation, which really comes down to the results they generate from the actions they take on a recurring basis.

So what do you do when you are not getting the results you need? The simplistic answer is just do more, but more what; if you run a steakhouse and you are not selling enough steak you don't just buy and cook more. If you were a doctor and your patient did not respond to medication you don't just prescribe more as that could be malpractice.

For a Sales Team, you have to examine what you are doing on a daily basis that leads to sales results. Look closely at what you do that are activities that lead to a sale; here are two simple examples.

1. When you sit and wait for the phone to ring or the email to come in, you are totally out of control of our business. You do not want to do any more of that.

2. When you specifically target a prospect or customer to understand their world, their challenges and their issues and from that work to find ways to help by delivering your technologies and solutions, that puts you in control of your business. You definitely want to do more of that.

Have the courage to be honest with yourself and make the decision to focus on adjusting your personal sales behaviours to get you on track to meeting or exceeding your targets and expectations.

E = Execute With Excellence

Planning is important. Taking action is important. Executing your plan with specific actions is fundamental to generating results! Action implies activity; execution implies focused and targeted activity. As you move ahead with your business planning for the next fiscal period you must be in sync philosophically and committed practically to executing against your plan on a daily and weekly basis. You should expect to be measured and managed by how well you execute the plan and you should embrace the responsibility and accept total accountability for what results are achieved. If you do not follow through with this execution, then you are effectively admitting your success is hope based rather than plan based.

As I have been known to say, you need to Plan Meticulously and Execute Brilliantly!

R = Results Lead To Rewards And Recognition

It should come as no surprise that really good sales people tend to be highly results oriented and look to be rewarded and recognized for their efforts. The other truth is results do not just happen without significant time and effort.

THINK TO WIN

Visualize Success

'If you think you can you can and if you think you can't you're right.' Winning with purpose is about seeing and believing you can win well before you start. For Sales, it is making a call, conducting a meeting or closing a piece of business with the intent to be successful.

Be Ready For Anything

No outcome you encounter should be 'unexpected' as that just means you were not properly prepared. Preparing includes working through what you believe all the possible outcomes to be and having a way to overcome or handle them. The other real benefit of doing this is you eliminate the emotional factor of surprise which allows you to better respond and not just react to a situation that is not going as you had anticipated.

Stay In The Moment

It seems heavily overused but that is because it is so true. Focus on executing your best call, your best meeting, your best follow up, your best whatever it is you are doing right now. Avoid the trap of getting way ahead of yourself and your business and you will also avoid the added pressure of having to totally depend on winning each and every opportunity.

Be Yourself

In the final analysis you must be completely genuine with your customers and coworkers and the simplest way to do that is to be yourself. It speaks to integrity, credibility and trustworthiness which can all be 'sensed' in certain circumstances by other people.

THE ART AND SCIENCE OF CHANGE

Without Change There Can Be No Growth

This ties directly back to the old adage that 'if you just keep doing what you have always done, you will just keep getting what you have always gotten'. That might work for some, but your business plan probably targets growth and that means you have to do some things differently than before to achieve the success desired. Too many people look at change as a bad thing when the reality is that change is fundamental to all improvement. The sooner you not just accept but embrace change, the sooner you will be able to capitalize on the benefits that come from managed and disciplined change.

Change For The Sake Of Change Is A Waste Of Time

Although I am a committed believer in effecting change where and when necessary, I do not subscribe to the notion that there has to be change simply to have change. Making changes can cost time, effort and money and so change must be very carefully thought out before implementing. I suspect you have all had the experience of doing something a certain way that worked and in an attempt to make it 'better' a change was made only to make it worse and then you had to change back to the old way. Many people will focus on these 'bad' changes as a reason to resist all change and that too would be a serious mistake. Where warranted, change can be a massively positive thing.

Constantly Evaluate And Make Minor Changes
Be Evolutionary And Not Revolutionary

Change should be a constant based on minor or incremental course corrections that accumulate over time based on practical experience. You should always be asking "how can I do that better?" Every once in a while you might realize that specific activity or action cannot be done better because every time you do it you get the expected results. In that case, the question should simply be "how can I do more of the same and get more of the same results?" The reality is that most of the time there is room for improvement, even if on a very small scale. By accepting the need for that improvement and more importantly implementing that improvement, you are actually demonstrating responsibility and accountability for our actions and results.

Change Is Inevitable, Suffering Is Optional

You have all heard that 'Change is the only True Constant'.[13] As has been said countless times, the sooner you accept and embrace change, the happier and less stressed you will be.

MAKING AND KEEPING COMMITMENTS

Commitment Is Doing What you Said You Would Do Long After the Emotion You Said It With Has Left You!

It is so easy to simply say, in the heat or passion of the moment, that you are committed to doing something. It is much more difficult days or weeks later to stay the course and remain totally committed.

The Hell Or High Water Story

I am sure most of you have heard this story but it is worth repeating. There was a big flash flood and two young boys were sitting on a garage roof watching all the stuff float by in the high flood waters. One boy says to the other "that is really odd – that straw hat is going back and forth across the current and not floating away." The other boy responded "that is not odd at all. Last night at supper my Dad said tomorrow morning he was going to cut the grass, come hell or high water!" Now that is commitment!

The Breakfast Story

Again, I am sure most of you have heard this story about a standard bacon and eggs breakfast; the chicken is involved but the hog is committed!! Sort of reminds you of the old adage that 'everyone wants to go to heaven but nobody really wants to do what it takes to get there – die'!

THE POWER OF PASSION

Ignorance On Fire Is Often Better Than Knowledge On Ice!

Some might take exception to this quote but the point I am making is really quite simple; don't wait to be an expert to conduct a meeting but rather just get out there and do it! You all know of sales guys who seem to know nothing and yet are exceeding their targets and the 'veterans' will make comments like "that will come to an end soon", but does it have to?

There is no question you sometimes require specific information about a technology or solution to be able to answer a question or complete a follow up. You also know that can be effectively managed directly by deferring the question or getting one of your product specialists or experts connected to support you. Find the balance that works for you; that blending of passion and precision that carries customers along with you, gets them to open up and creates opportunities to find and win business.

Avoid Hype And Hyperbole

You have all met the sales types who are so hyped up you almost have to scrape them off the ceiling to have a real discussion with them. There is no place in business for hype, exaggerations or false claims. The passion you need to exhibit should just be there; your conviction that comes across in your conversations, the confidence that shows in your eyes and the strength that carries over in your handshake. You need your customers to be saying to themselves things like "I really like this guy. He believes in his company and his products and he is honest and forthright; I can do business with him."

Passion Comes From Belief

When you believe in yourself, when you believe in your Company and when you believe in your solutions, your passion will be there. By itself passion will not generate opportunities or POs but it will give you the strength to move ahead, deal with the natural adversity you face every day and be so much more successful than you might otherwise be.

To me it really is that simple.

BEGIN WITH THE END IN MIND[16]

It Is Hard To Drive Forward Looking Through The Rear View Mirror!

So say your last quarter is over, for better or worse. It is now time to forget what happened and focus on the new quarter. Take the time and work through your pipeline. Ask yourself if you really have enough business in the 'funnel' to meet or exceed your target and to create the momentum necessary to catch up what was missed previously and build for what follows. As a minimum, I would recommend your pipeline have at least three to four times the total revenue potential to what you need; anything less and you risk and depend far too much on a couple of key deals.

The More You Put Into It, The More You Put Into It!

The more you have at risk, the harder you will work to make sure you do not fail. The problem with this is that I do not recommend you work hard because you have to, I hope you work hard because you WANT to. It is a sad state of affairs when you measure your success by your lack of failure. At the end of the day, I want you to be able to say you had a great day because of the quality of your customer interactions and you received a PO and not because you did not have any problems to deal with.

Be inspired and motivated to roll up your sleeves and get back to basics. You all know the adage 'you cannot get blood from a stone'; you have to systematically reflect on whether the accounts you are servicing are going to generate the revenue you need. The only way to do this is to go back to your business plans and develop detailed 'tactical' plans for identifying and developing the opportunities to fill the pipeline and give you the confidence your target is achievable. If those accounts are not going to generate the revenue, then you have no choice but to create new accounts by methodically examining key verticals and take the necessary action to get things going. This is not easy but it can be very rewarding given time and focused effort.

The Best Plan Never Survives The First Customer Contact

No matter how well you plan and prepare for your next key customer contact, it is not at all uncommon that something completely unexpected happens. It is your ability to handle and manage those situations that may ultimately determine your success. Good planning means developing contingencies that allow you to overcome challenges as they occur. Note I did not say 'unforeseen' or 'non-forecasted' challenges because it is through meticulous planning that you figure out all the 'what ifs' that might arise. Being prepared allows you to respond and not react when your customer does something different than you expected. In advance of meetings, it can be very worthwhile to practise your presentation and role play or brainstorm anticipated issues and concerns so you are truly ready.

Are You A Hunter Or A Farmer?

For a very long time, Sales people have been categorized as either Hunters or Farmers. Hunters focus on landing new accounts and closing big deals. Farmers are more focused on maintaining existing accounts. Hunters get turned on by the next conquest. Farmers provide better service levels for stable accounts. Hunters have very different sales personalities than Farmers. Most companies expect you to be able to do both and one cannot be favoured at the expense of the other.

What is common to both is the critical need to develop and nurture relationships. Whether you are doing business development hunter type activities or account management farmer type activities, you should always be looking to expand the number and quality of relationships you own. Remember you need to be continually adding more opportunities and whether you are a Hunter or Farmer, this is still a key task each and every day.

KEYS TO BUILDING A STRONG RELATIONSHIP

Seek Out Common Ground

Work at developing a sales relationship the same way you would build a social relationship, by finding common ground between you and your prospect or customer. It is okay if the relationship is purely business and develops based on successful transactions, but it is better if your customers see you more as a trusted and respected advisor assisting them to solve their challenges. Remember that people who have shared experiences, hobbies, sports, etcetera find it easier to communicate and spend time together.

Every Call And Contact Should Be To Advance The Relationship

Of primary importance here is the perspective that you need to move away from a transactional based model to a relationship based model. If all you care about is getting and fulfilling an order, you might need to adjust your thinking and attitude. Developing and sustaining long term mutually beneficial relationships means there has to be some give and take and there will be some bumps along the way. Even if you are results driven and in the end that is how you are compensated and your performance is judged, you must also be sensitive that if your customers see you as only interested in them when they have a PO in hand they will soon start to look elsewhere for their trusted advisors.

To build this type of relationship takes a lot of work and a lot of direct contact. You will need multiple phone calls and equally important, you must have face to face meetings as often as can be managed. Even if you have a great relationship with a customer, you still have to get in front of them personally on a regular basis. Get them out of the office or cubicle, which is where many live all day, and they will be much more open to discussing what is really going on in their professional lives.

Price Versus Value

There is no question that price is a significant factor in a procurement decision but you also know that when the only conversation you are having with a customer is about price, you are probably having the wrong conversation and maybe with the wrong person. When you have a real relationship with a customer who truly understands the value proposition you offer, then price diminishes in overall relative importance. One of the most critical responsibilities you have in Sales is to deliver the value proposition and ensure the customer fully appreciates your offering, your skills and abilities and your commitment to excellence.

You cannot just play lip service to this; you must under promise and over deliver and you must execute brilliantly on all steps of the sales process. Individually, you must take complete ownership and responsibility for your customers and ensure their needs are met and their challenges are resolved. Doing this creates value and strengthens the relationship.

Honesty, Integrity And Professionalism

Most customers will see this as a black and white issue but to my way of thinking, you do not just want to be seen as honest or professional but you want to be known and talked about as being at the top of their list when these descriptors are discussed. Under no circumstances do you want to be found or even perceived to be less 'than' in any of these, as it is almost impossible to recover or rehabilitate your reputation once tarnished. Also remember it is not just you personally that is under constant evaluation by your customers but the Company as well, so everyone has a role to play in ensuring you meet or exceed standards.

Building a relationship can be a long and complex process but it does start with the first meeting and impression. I personally believe most people will give you the benefit of the doubt in the beginning and allow your actions over time to shape or reinforce their views and opinions. I am

252

convinced one of the key things you can do to build a really strong relationship is to 'do what you said you would do when you said you would do it' but I urge caution in not making commitments to deliverables that the Company cannot meet, whether it is for quotes or products or support. To use an old adage, in your haste to get the business, Sales has to be really cautious you do not 'write cheques you cannot cash'!

Immediate Actions

You must take the time to seriously examine each customer and ask yourself a couple of key questions
1. How good is my relationship with this customer?
2. What can I do to make it better as soon as possible?
The quality of the relationship you have with a customer should allow you to sit down with them and identify what key problems and issues they face that can turn into funded projects you can help them with. This type of information is invaluable; it allows you to develop a unique plan for each customer, forms the basis for your opportunities and feeds directly into your ongoing business planning process.

Section 4 – My Top 10

I was taught that when you do a presentation you should always start by telling your audience what you are going to talk to them about, then you go ahead and do the talking and then you finish by telling them what you told them. To finish this book, I am going to highlight my top 10 list. It will be a combination of principles, ideas and thoughts that resonate with me and that I work hard to practise each and every day. Most have been discussed a couple times already but they are all worth reviewing one last time. It was quite difficult to pare the list down to 10 but here they are.

NOTHING I DO IS URGENT BUT
I DO EVERYTHING WITH A SENSE OF URGENCY!

Easy to say and very tough to live by. You can be in the middle of an important project or task when the phone rings and like most people, you allow that interruption to now be an urgent priority that must be dealt with immediately. What is really interesting is that you make answering the phone the priority often without knowing who is calling or about what; it could be a telemarketer or it could be a friend just wanting to chat.

Human nature is that, when faced with a number of different tasks, you tend to do the easiest ones first and leave the tough ones to the end. I do not advocate doing the tough tasks first, rather I recommend you take a few minutes to prioritize based on what is most important and not just what is most urgent. Sometimes urgency and importance are in conflict and it can be quite challenging to set aside something that is urgent but not really important. What invariably happens if you do not get his under control is that you only work on things that are urgent and maybe you are not always doing your best work given the urgency!

UNDER PROMISE AND OVER DELIVER!

Especially in Sales, this one is critical. Mess up on a promise to a customer and it can take a long time to recover. If you have a long standing relationship you can get away with an 'oops' now and then but if this is a new account you have to be perfectly on track the first few times. It is like the old adage of 'fool me once shame on you but fool me twice shame on me'.

One of the real dangers is when salespeople make promises to get the order, sometimes knowing full well they cannot meet delivery dates and then put huge pressure on the rest of the Company to step up and make it happen on time. Take the extra time before making any promises to make sure you can meet or exceed customer expectations and then hold the organization to what has been agreed and committed to.

PLAN METICULOUSLY, EXECUTE FLAWLESSLY!

In spite of this one being 'beaten to death' throughout this book, it deserves repeating again. I do not believe you can be too prepared but do not fall into the trap of not having planned enough as an excuse for not executing. There is such a thing as 'paralysis by analysis' which is just another form of procrastination. Plans should be documented and if a team or a group are involved, be very clear on who is responsible for what and by when and ensure everyone steps up and meets their obligations.

Also remember that a good plan that is executed in a timely fashion is often much better than a perfect plan executed late or not at all; this is an extension of the 'best is the enemy of the good' philosophy.

COMMITMENT IS DOING WHAT YOU SAID YOU WOULD DO LONG AFTER THE EMOTION YOU SAID IT WITH HAS LEFT YOU!

This one is about as self-evident as it gets, yet it is still way too common a problem that people raise their hand to volunteer to do something in the heat of the moment and then later do not follow through on that commitment. Regardless of whether they are too busy or just plain forget, their lack of following through can leave you and the company at risk.

THE 3-LEGGED STOOL OF ACCOUNTABILITY, RESPONSIBILITY AND AUTHORITY

Unless you have all three, you are most likely predisposed to fail just like the stool cannot stand on two legs. It really is as simple as that.

CHANGE IS INEVITABLE, SUFFERING IS OPTIONAL!

Change must be managed, it must be necessary and it must be well intentioned to be successful. The sooner you become an agent of change and embrace it for all the right reasons, the sooner you will not suffer.

SALES IS THE WORST PAID EASY WORK AND THE BEST PAID HARD WORK YOU WILL EVER DO!

If it was easy anyone could do it. Some of the highest paid are true professional sales people who work relentlessly to be the best they can be. They are students of their craft, do not accept mediocrity and never give up.

THE MORE YOU PUT INTO IT THE MORE YOU PUT INTO IT!

When you are proverbially 'all in' and fully committed you do not easily give up or walk away. When faced with obstacles you either find a way around or make one. If you cannot accept risk or accountability or responsibility do not expect to win big or earn big; the greater the challenges and problems you solve the more value you bring to an organization.

IF YOU ARE NOT PREPARED TO GIVE UP WHAT YOU'VE GOT TO GET WHAT YOU REALLY WANT YOU WILL JUST HAVE TO KEEP WHAT YOU'VE GOT WHETHER YOU LIKE IT OR NOT!

If you are not happy with your career or income or relationships or whatever, then do something about it or quit complaining and accept it.

The great news is that you really can become anything you choose to if you are prepared to put in the work and effort necessary.

MANAGEMENT IS THE SCIENCE OF REACTION
LEADERSHIP IS THE ART OF ACTION

It has been a privilege for me to share this book with you. I hope that you have been able to take away one or more ideas, strategies, tactics or thoughts that will help you become a better manager and better leader or better person. I wish you the best of success in all your future endeavours!

Section 5 -

Notes

Often attributed to John Burke is the quote "if you steal from one author, it plagiarism; if you steal from many, it's research." I have often joked to audiences that was I do is 'practise applied plagiarism based on pure research'. Over the years I have read countless books on sales, business and personal development, watched and listened to many speakers and in the process I have accumulated a significant number of quotes and clichés and sometimes do not remember where it might have originated. Many times throughout this book I have quoted others and in many cases I have credited them in the main body but I also offer a list here of all the others that I could find specific references to. Many of the quotes and clichés I use have become part of everyday jargon and in many cases detailed internet searches could not identify the originator but if anyone identifies one or more I have missed attributing correctly please let me know and any future releases will be appropriately updated.

1. Bennis, Warren and Nanus, Leaders: The Strategies for Taking Charge, Harper and Row, 1985

2. Attributed to John Lydgate, British Monk and Poet, 1370-1451

3. Attributed to both Benjamin Franklin, Founding Father of the United States and John L Beckley, 1st Librarian of the United States Congress 1757-1807

4. Attributed to Andrew Carnegie, US Industrialist and Philantropist, 1835-1919

5. Mark Victor Hansen and Jack Canfield in their Chicken Soup For The Soul book series

6. Attributed to Henry Ford, US Industrialist, 1863-1947

7. From the movie Star Wars The Empire Strikes Back, produced by Lucasfilm Ltd, 1980

8. Comments by President Barack Obama, October 5th 2011

9. Taken from Wikipedia.org website on the subject of Teamwork

10. Attributed to Voltaire in his poem La Beguelle in 1770

11. Attibuted to Eleanor Roosevelt, US First Lady 1933-1945

12. Attributed to Thomas Edison, US Inventor and Businessman, 1847-1931

13. Attributed to Heradiths of Ephesus, Greek Philosopher 535-475 BC

14. Attributed to Albert Einstein, German born Physicist 1879-1955

15. Attributed to William Shakespear, Playright in Julius Caesar 1569-1616

16. From the book by Stephen Covey, The 7 Habits of Highly Effective People, 1989

17. Attributed to John Bytheway, US Author, 1962-Present

18. Attributed to US General Creighton Abrams Jr, 1914-1974

19. Attributed to Lao Tzu, Chinese Poet and Philosopher, 571-531 BC

20. From the book by Richard Nelson, What Color is Your Parachute, Ten Speed Press, 1970

21. Trademark of Nike Inc

22. Attributed to Lucius Annaeus Seneca, Roman Philosopher, 4 BC – 65 AD

23. Attributed to Tony Robbins from his Lessons in Mastery Series based on the Japanese word Kaizen

24. From the book by Jim Rohn, The Art of Exceptional Living, Simon and Shuster, 1994

25. From the book by Napoleon Hill, Think and Grow Rich, The Ralston Society, 1937

26. From Wikipedia.org

27. Attributed to Arnold Bennett, Film Writer, 1867-1931